HOW EVERYTHING CAN COLLAPSE

To all those who feel fear, sadness and anger.
To all those who act as if we were all in the same boat.
To the 'rough weather networks' inspired by Joanna Macy,
that swarm and connect.

HOW EVERYTHING CAN COLLAPSE

A Manual for Our Times

Pablo Servigne and Raphaël Stevens

Translated by Andrew Brown

polity

First published in French as *Comment tout peut s'effondrer: Petit manuel de collapsologie à l'usage des générations présentes* © Éditions du Seuil, 2015
This English edition © Polity Press, 2020

13

Polity Press
65 Bridge Street
Cambridge CB2 1UR, UK

Polity Press
101 Station Landing
Suite 300
Medford, MA 02155, USA

ISBN-13: 978-1-5095-4138-6
ISBN-13: 978-1-5095-4139-3 – paperback

A catalogue record for this book is available from the British Library.

Library of Congress Cataloging-in-Publication Data
Names: Servigne, Pablo, author. | Stevens, Raphaël, author. | Brown, Andrew (Literary translator), translator.
Title: How everything can collapse : a manual for our times / Pablo Servigne and Raphaël Stevens ; translated by Andrew Brown.
Other titles: Comment tout peut s'effondrer. English.
Description: Cambridge, UK ; Medford, MA : Polity, [2020] | "First published in French as Comment tout peut s'effondrer: Petit manuel de collapsologie à l'usage des générations présentes © Éditions du Seuil, 2015." | Includes bibliographical references. | Summary: "A brave book that confronts directly the very real possibility that our civilization will collapse"-- Provided by publisher.
Identifiers: LCCN 2019045588 (print) | LCCN 2019045589 (ebook) | ISBN 9781509541386 (hardback) | ISBN 9781509541393 (paperback) | ISBN 9781509541409 (epub)
Subjects: LCSH: Regression (Civilization) | Crises (Philosophy) | Climatic changes--Effect of human beings on. | Global environmental change--Forecasting. | Forecasting.
Classification: LCC CB151 .S4713 2020 (print) | LCC CB151 (ebook) | DDC 909--dc23
LC record available at https://lccn.loc.gov/2019045588
LC ebook record available at https://lccn.loc.gov/2019045589

Typeset in 10.75pt on 14pt Janson by
Servis Filmsetting Limited, Stockport, Cheshire
Printed and bound in Great Britain by TJ Books Limited

For further information on Polity, visit our website:
politybooks.com

Ecological catastrophes looming worldwide at a time of demographic growth, inequalities due to the local scarcity of water, the end of cheap energy, the increasing scarcity of many minerals, the undermining of biodiversity, soil erosion and pollution, extreme climatic events and so on will produce the greatest inequalities between those able to protect themselves from these problems (at least for a time), and those who will suffer from them. These catastrophes will undermine the geopolitical balance, and trigger conflict. The extent of the social disasters they may cause has led, in the past, to the disappearance of whole societies. This, alas, is an objective historical reality. [...] Once the collapse of the species appears as a conceivable possibility, the state of emergency will have no time for our slow and complex processes of deliberation. The West will be panic-stricken, and will transgress its values of freedom and justice.

Michel Rocard (former French Prime Minister), Dominique Bourg (Professor at the Faculty of Geosciences and Environment, University of Lausanne) and Floran Augagneur (Professor of the Philosophy of Ecology at the Institute of Political Studies in Paris), 2011

There is some probability that oil production will peak around 2010, and this will have consequences for security within fifteen to thirty years. [...] In the medium term, the global economic system as well as each national market economy could collapse.

Report of the Bundeswehr (German Army), 2010

The following risks are identified with great certainty: [...] 3. Systemic risks due to extreme weather phenomena leading to the breakdown of infrastructure networks and essential services such as electricity, the water supply, and health and emergency services. [...] 5. Risk of food insecurity and disruption of food systems.

Fifth Report of the Intergovernmental Panel on Climate Change, 2014

Our global civilization today is on an economic path that is environmentally unsustainable, a path that is leading us toward economic decline and eventual collapse.

Lester Brown (founder of Worldwatch Institute, founder and president of the Earth Policy Institute), *Plan B 2.0*, 2006

Probably the greatest agreement among scholars, though, is that the failing civilizations suffered from growing hubris and overconfidence: the belief that their capabilities after many earlier tests would always rise to the occasion and that growing signs of weakness could be ignored as pessimistic.

Jeremy Grantham (investor, co-founder of Grantham Mayo van Otterloo (GMO), one of the largest fund managers on the planet), 2013

Systems often hold longer than we think, but they end up by collapsing much faster than we imagine.

Ken Rogoff (former Chief Economist of the International Monetary Fund), 2012

Can humanity avoid a starvation-driven collapse? Yes, we can – though we currently put the odds at just 10 per cent. As dismal as that sounds, we believe that, for the benefit of future generations, it is worth struggling to make it 11 per cent.

Paul R. Ehrlich and Anne H. Ehrlich (Professors of Biology at Stanford University), 2013

Contents

Part III   Collapsology

Foreword:
Candles Only Shine Within Darkness

When we read the latest news of disasters, extreme weather, changes to our planet and scientists' warnings, it is natural to feel unease, even fear. Some of you may have even suffered direct consequences of climate chaos, such as failing harvests, forest fires or political unrest from prolonged drought. If so, I want to recognize at the outset that my own anxiety about the future is nothing compared to what you have already been through. And that people like me can learn from you. Yet all of us are now being affected by the climate crisis in some way, whether it is from rising prices or the rise of extremism as people feel unsafe and uncertain. Many of us have busy lives and obligations, which means that although we sense this growing danger, it is difficult to turn towards it. Without time to delve into this issue, how can I know what the real situation is? What are the issues to consider or the options we have? Who should we talk to about it all?

These are the difficulties for even starting a conversation about the breakdown or collapse of the society we live in due to climate change. It is why this book is so helpful in starting the conversation. The first step in engaging with this topic is to allow yourself to consider 'what if' the future is as difficult for humanity, everywhere, as some of the scholars are now saying. If you do allow that outlook into your consciousness, then you are embarking on a bizarre ride.

Well, at least it has been a bizarre ride for me! Every person's journey on this topic will be different, especially when the months go by and the impacts will worsen while more of our friends, colleagues and neighbours will wake up to our predicament.

First, there is the self-doubt.

Is it really so bad? Might someone or some technology be able to stop it? Is it helpful to have such a negative outlook on the future? Does that mean I have a negative view on human nature? Will I be able to cope with life if I accept such a bleak view of our future? Such doubts are natural, even before we begin to talk to others about our perspective.

Second, there are painful emotions.

Once one has accepted that our societies will break down or collapse, there can be great sorrow, fear and confusion. How did we do this to life on Earth? Who are we as a species? What could I do to help the people I love? What could I do to help humanity and nature? How bad will it get? Where and when? It can be normal to experience moments of panic. Some of us can also feel like blaming someone, as anger provides a momentary release from our fear. We might also jump from one simple answer or preoccupation to another. Yet none of these mental habits will distract us from the underlying pain for very long.

Third, there is a sense of isolation.

Who can I talk to about this? Will they think I am overly anxious or depressed? Will they be traumatized, so I will feel bad about triggering their pain? How can I talk about this with young people? Where is there advice or guidance on how to be with this perspective, let alone how to start changing my life as a result?

Fourth, there is a new community.

Suddenly we find people we can talk to about the situation and share ideas about how we live with it and what to do next. I have experienced the excitement of meeting people in this way. Yet also there is pain because the joy of connection then increases the sense of forthcoming loss. As the situation we connect with is so challenging, emotions can run high. More community means more of every human emotion.

Fifth, there is the backlash.

What did he say about me? Why would she say that it is immoral to have concluded how bad our situation is? Why is there such anger in their criticism? What are they hiding from themselves? Shall I just disengage in conversations with them and live my own truth? If I do, does that mean I am giving up on engaging in society to try and reduce harm? Why should I have to do that?

Sixth, there is the transformation.

But there is not one path of transformation. You will have your experience and come to your own conclusions. One reason I introduced a 'deep adaptation' framework was to open up conversations on the myriad of potential responses once we believe that the breakdown or collapse of our civilization is likely or inevitable within our own lifetimes. Your inner and outer transformation could be supported through new-found community and resources like this book, but ultimately you need to find your own path in what is completely new territory for humanity.

Seventh, there is dying well.

Although we all die, modern society seems to hide this away from our daily consciousness. An awakening to our climate predicament is an awakening to our common mortality and impermanence more generally. Often we talk of responding to climate chaos, including how it can transform our lives, can focus on what we can do differently, where there is an assumption it is only about how we live differently. That is not enough. Instead, we can ask what dying well might look like for us. What do I want to look back on? How do I want to approach death? What might I die for? How do I feel about what happens, if anything, after death? How might I help others to approach the death of themselves and others more consciously and lovingly?

I share with you some of these steps to map some of the new reality for people who are collapse-aware. I think I do that because I want to belong. I want to engage in conversations where we weave new stories of being in these troubling times. That is why I welcome the work of people like Pablo Servigne, Raphaël Stevens and Gauthier Chapelle. Because the first step towards opening those new conversations that create new stories and belonging is to break the taboo around climate-induced collapse. When I wrote my paper on 'deep adaptation' to imminent climate collapse, I was not aware that Pablo and Raphaël suggested calling this nascent field of scholarship 'collapsology'. There certainly wasn't such a field within my own area of expertise. As I explained in my paper, it was taboo. Since the paper went viral around the world, I discovered people exploring this terrain and changing their lives. Thousands of people were getting in touch, and so I encouraged them all to connect with each other by launching a Deep Adaptation Forum. We are mostly an English-language network, yet I am keen to learn from the work in France and elsewhere. This book will help you to discover that work and join an ever-widening conversation about what to do in the face of this most difficult predicament.

It requires some courage to break a taboo. It requires some courage to make people aware of darkness that they had not seen before or had turned away from. Especially when that darkness is not only in the changing climate and the institutions that have damaged our world but also within us. Because we have all participated in both the creation of this disaster and the ignoring of it. Or have been satisfied with ineffectual action that provided us with a believable myth of being a good person. As such, climate chaos is an invitation to go deeper into self-reflection and learn about why we have participated in such destruction. From that inquiry, we may find ways of living that avoid making matters worse. Bringing attention to the darkness around us, ahead of us and inside of us is essential if we are then to light candles of wisdom. People who are bringing attention to the darkness are also lighting candles of wisdom. Candles only shine within darkness. As more candles are lit, so we can see each other anew. We can connect with what is burning inside our hearts and live from that truth more fully than before.

Professor Jem Bendell, author of *Deep Adaptation*

Acknowledgements

Thanks are due to Christophe Bonneuil, Gauthier Chapelle, Élise Monette, Olivier Alléra, Daniel Rodary, Jean Chanel, Yves Cochet and Flore Boudet for their attentive, courageous and benevolent readings, with a special mention for Yves Cochet, who offered us the postscript, and our editor Christophe Bonneuil, who believed in our ideas and our project and who guided us with unfailing patience. Thanks also to Sophie Lhuillier and Charles Olivero at Le Seuil for their close and patient work. The idea for the final poem goes back to our brother Gauthier Chapelle, an essential link in the networks in these difficult times, and now a seasoned collapsologist. Thanks also to Agnès Sinaï, Yves Cochet (again) and to friends of the Institut Momentum for creating a place and opportunities for such fertile exchanges around these taboo topics, and to our friends at *Barricade*, *Etopia*, *Nature & Progrès*, *BeTransition*, *Imagine* and *Réfractions* for allowing these ideas to live before we wrote our manuscript. The material conditions of research and writing were particularly difficult at the end of 2014, and so we feel an immense gratitude for our partners, families, friends and neighbours who supported this birth by creating the right material and psychological conditions for us. Thank you, therefore, to Élise, Stéphanie, Nelly and Michel, Chantal and Pierre, Brigitte and Philippe, Monique, Benoît and Caroline, Antoine and Sandrine, Thomas and Noëlle, Philippe and Martine,

Pierre-Antoine and Gwendoline, and the B'z! Finally, thank you to everyone who came to talk to us after the conferences, workshops and training sessions and who encouraged us to continue this research.

Introduction

We'll Definitely Need to Tackle the Subject One of These Days ...

Crises, disasters, collapses, decline ... Apocalypse can be read between the lines of the daily news from across the world. While some disasters are real enough and supply our newspapers with their news items – plane crashes, hurricanes, floods, the decline in the number of bees, slumps in the stock market, and wars – is it justifiable to suggest that our society is 'heading for disaster', to announce a 'global planetary crisis', or to point to a 'sixth mass extinction of species'?

It has become a paradox: we have to face this deluge of disasters in the media, but we're unable to talk explicitly about the really *big* catastrophes without being called alarmists or 'catastrophists'! Everyone, for example, knew that the IPCC had issued a new report on climate change in 2014, but did we see any real debate about these new climate scenarios and their implications in terms of social change? No, of course not. Too catastrophist.

Perhaps we're tired of bad news. And in any case, hasn't the end of the world always been looming? Isn't taking the darkest possible view of the future a typically European or western piece of narcissism? Isn't catastrophism a new opium of the people, distilled by ecological ayatollahs and scientists in need of funding? Come on, everybody, give it a bit of welly – we'll soon have put paid to the 'crisis'!

But perhaps we don't actually know how to talk about disasters – the real ones, those that last, those that don't fit into the news cycle. After all, let's admit it: we're facing some serious problems to do with the environment, energy, climate change, geopolitics, and social and economic issues, problems that are now at a point of no return. Few people say it, but all these 'crises' are interconnected, influencing and intensifying each other. We now have a huge bundle of evidence suggesting that we're up against growing systemic instabilities that pose a serious threat to the ability of several human populations – and indeed human beings as a whole – to maintain themselves in a sustainable environment.

Collapse?

It's not the end of the world, nor the Apocalypse. Nor is it a simple crisis from which we can emerge unscathed or a one-off disaster that we can forget after a few months, like a tsunami or a terrorist attack. A collapse is 'the process at the end of which basic needs (water, food, housing, clothing, energy, etc.) can no longer be provided [at a reasonable cost] to a majority of the population by services under legal supervision'.[1] So it's a large-scale, irreversible process – just like the end of the world, admittedly, except that it's not the end! It looks as if the consequences will last for a long time, and we'll need to live through them. And one thing is certain: we don't have the means to know what they will consist of. On the other hand, if our 'basic needs' are affected, it is easy to imagine that the situation *could* become immeasurably catastrophic.

But how far will it all extend? Who will be affected? The poorest countries? France? Europe? All the rich countries? The industrialized world? Western civilization? All of humankind? Or even, as some scientists are predicting, the vast majority of living species? There are no clear answers to these questions, but one thing is certain: none of these possibilities can be ruled out. The 'crises' we are experiencing affect all these categories: for example, the end of oil concerns the whole of the industrialized world (but not the small traditional peasant societies that have been left out by globalization), whereas climate change threatens human beings as a whole, as well as a large proportion of living species.

Scientific publications that envisage global catastrophes and an increasing probability of collapse are becoming more numerous and better supported by the evidence. The Royal Society published an article by Paul and Anne Ehrlich on this subject in 2013, leaving little doubt about the outcome.[2] The consequences of the global environmental changes viewed as likely in the second half of the twenty-first century are becoming all too evident in the light of ever more precise and overwhelming numerical data. The climate is heating up, biodiversity is collapsing, pollution is ubiquitous and becoming persistent, the economy risks going into cardiac arrest at every moment, social and geopolitical tensions are growing, etc. It is not unusual to see decision makers at the highest level, and official reports from major institutions (the World Bank, the armed forces, the IPCC, banks, NGOs, etc.), discussing the possibility of collapse, or what Prince Charles calls 'suicide on a grand scale'.[3]

More broadly, the Anthropocene is the name given to this new geological era, namely our own present.[4] We – human beings – emerged from the Holocene, a time of remarkable climatic stability that lasted about twelve thousand years and allowed the emergence of agriculture and civilization. In recent decades, humans (or at least many of them, in growing numbers) have become capable of upsetting the large biogeochemical cycles of the Earth system, thereby creating a new era of profound and unpredictable change.

However, these findings and figures are 'cold'. How does all this affect our daily lives? Don't you feel that there is a huge gap that needs to be filled, a link that needs to be forged between these great scientific statements, so rigorous and all encompassing, and the everyday life that gets lost in the details, in the clutter of the unexpected and the heat of our emotions? It's precisely this gap that our book seeks to fill, drawing a connection between the Anthropocene and your gut feelings. For that purpose, we have chosen the notion of 'collapse' because it allows us to play on several registers, tackling both the rates of biodiversity decline and the emotions related to disasters, and to discuss the risk of famine. This is a concept that involves both popular images drawn from cinema (who can fail to visualize Mel Gibson out in the desert, armed with a pump shotgun?) and narrowly focused scientific reports; it allows us to approach different temporalities (from the urgency of daily life to geological time) while comfortably navigating between past and future; and it allows us to draw a connection between, for example, the Greek social and economic crisis and the large-scale disappearance of populations of birds and insects in China and Europe. In short, it is this concept that brings to tangible life the notion of the Anthropocene.

And yet, in media and intellectual circles, the question of collapse is not taken seriously. The notorious computer bug that threatened to strike in 2000, and the 'Mayan event' of 21 December 2012, put paid to the possibility of any serious and factual argument. Anyone who publicly mentions a 'collapse' is seen as announcing the Apocalypse, and relegated to the narrow category of those 'credulous believers' in the 'irrational' who have 'always existed'. End of story. Time to change the subject! The process of automatically dismissing such talk – a dismissal which, as it happens, itself appears truly irrational – has left public debate in such a state of intellectual disrepair that it is no longer possible to express oneself without adopting one of two simplistic standpoints which often border on the ridiculous. On the one hand, we are subjected to apocalyptic, survivalist or pseudo-Mayan language; on the other hand, we have to endure the 'progressive' denials of Luc Ferry, Claude Allègre, Pascal Bruckner and their ilk. These two postures, both frenziedly clinging to their respective myths (the myth of the Apocalypse vs the myth of progress), reinforce each other, view each other as a scarecrow and share a phobia for dignified and respectful debate. All of this just reinforces the attitude of uninhibited collective denial that is such a prominent feature of our times.

The birth of 'collapsology'

Despite the high quality of some of the philosophical reflections on this topic,[5] the debate on collapse (or 'the end of *a* world') fails because of the absence of factual arguments. It is stuck in imaginary or philosophical speculation without any real factual grounding. The books dealing with collapse are usually too specialized, restricted by their point of view or discipline (archaeology, economics, ecology, etc.), while more systematic discussions are full of gaps. Jared Diamond's bestseller *Collapse*, for example, sticks to the archaeology, ecology and biogeography of ancient civilizations and does not address some of the essential questions of the current situation.[6] As for other popular books, they usually tackle the question by adopting a survivalist position (telling you how to make bows and arrows, or how to find drinking water in a world plagued by fire and the sword), giving the reader all the thrills of watching a zombie movie.

Not only do we lack any real inventory – or better, any systematic analysis – of the planet's economic and biophysical situation, but above all we lack an overview of what a collapse might look like, how it might be triggered and what it would imply in psychological, sociological and political terms *for the present generations*. We lack any real applied, transdisciplinary science of collapse.

We here propose, by drawing on information from many scattered works published across the world, to create the basics of what, with a certain self-deprecating irony, we have called 'collapsology' (from the Latin *collapsus*, 'a fallen mass'). The goal is not to indulge in the mere scientific pleasure of accumulating knowledge but rather to shed light on what is happening and might happen to us, in other words, to give meaning to events. It is also and above all a way of treating the subject as seriously as possible so that we can calmly discuss the policies that need to be implemented.

The issues that emerge whenever the word 'collapse' is so much as mentioned are many and varied. What do we know about the overall state of our Earth? Or the state of our civilization? Is a collapse in stock market prices comparable to a collapse in biodiversity? Can the conjunction and perpetuation of 'crises' actually drag our civilization into an inescapable whirlpool? How far can all this go? How long will it last? Will we manage to maintain our democratic reflexes? Can we live more or less peacefully through a 'civilized' collapse? Will the outcome inevitably be entirely negative?

Immersing ourselves in the word 'collapse', understanding its subtleties and nuances, distinguishing between fact and fantasy – these are some of the objectives of collapsology. We need to take this notion apart and conjugate it in different tenses to give it texture, detail, and nuance: we need, in short, to make of it a living and fully operational concept. Whether we are thinking of Mayan civilization, the Roman Empire or more recently the USSR, history shows us that there are varying degrees of collapse, and that, even if there are constants, each case is unique.

Moreover, the world is not uniform. The question of 'North–South relations' needs to be considered in a new light. An average American consumes a lot more resources and energy than an average African. However, the consequences of global heating will be far worse in countries close to the equator – precisely those which have emitted the least gas and contributed least to the greenhouse effect. It seems obvious that the temporality of a collapse will not be linear and its geography will not be homogeneous.

So this isn't a book that is meant to scare you. We will not be dealing with millenarian eschatology, nor with the potential astrophysical or tectonic events that could trigger a mass extinction of species of the kind the Earth saw sixty-five million years ago. We have enough to deal with when we look at what humans can do all by themselves. Nor is this a pessimistic book that doesn't believe in the future, nor a 'positive' book that minimizes the problem by providing 'solutions' in the last chapter. It's a book that attempts lucidly to set out the facts, to ask relevant questions, and to assemble a toolbox which will make it possible to grasp the subject other than through Hollywood disaster movies, the Mayan calendar or 'techno-bliss'. We are not just presenting a 'top ten' of the century's bad news stories, we are mainly proposing a theoretical framework for hearing about, understanding and welcoming all the small-scale initiatives that are already facing up to the 'post-carbon' world, initiatives that are emerging at breakneck speed.

Beware, this is a sensitive subject!

However, rationality alone is not enough to tackle such a subject. We have been interested in collapsology for some years now, and our experience – especially our meetings with the public – has taught us that facts and figures alone are not enough to give an adequate picture of the situation. We definitely need to add intuition, emotions and a certain ethics. Collapsology is not a neutral science detached from its object of study. 'Collapsologists' are directly affected by what they are studying. They cannot remain neutral anymore. They *must* not do so!

Taking such a path is a risky business. Collapse is a toxic subject that reaches right down into the core of your being. It's a huge shock, a sobering wake-up call. During these years of research, we have been submerged by waves of anxiety, anger and deep sadness before feeling, very gradually, a certain acceptance, and sometimes even hope and joy. By reading books on transition, such as Rob Hopkins's famous handbook,[7] we have been able to connect these emotions to the stages of mourning. We can mourn the loss of *one vision* of the future. Indeed, starting to understand and then to believe in the possibility of a collapse finally involves giving up on the future we had imagined. It means being forcibly deprived of the hopes, dreams and expectations that we had forged for ourselves since earliest childhood and those that we had nursed for our children. Accepting the possibility of a collapse means accepting the death of a future that was dear to us, a future that was reassuring, however irrational it might have been. What a wrench!

We have also had the unpleasant experience of seeing the anger of those close to us projecting itself onto us and crystallizing in us. This is a well-known phenomenon: in order to stave off bad news, we prefer to kill the messengers, the Cassandras and the whistle-blowers. But besides the fact that this does not solve the problem of collapse, we will warn the reader right now that we are not very fond of this kind of outcome.... Let's talk about collapse, but calmly. It's true that the possibility of a collapse shuts down certain futures dear to us; this comes as a real shock, but it opens up countless other futures, some surprisingly cheerful. The challenge, then, is to tame these new futures and make them viable.

In our first public interventions, we took care to deal only with figures and facts, to stay as objective as possible. Every time, the emotions of the audience surprised us. The more clearly the facts were set out, the stronger were people's emotions. We thought we were talking to people's heads and we were touching their hearts: sadness, tears, anxiety, resentment and outbursts of anger frequently erupted from the public. Our language gave words to intuitions that many people already had, and it struck a deep chord. In return, these reactions echoed our own feelings, which we had tried to conceal. After the lectures, the warm expressions of gratitude and enthusiasm were more numerous and above all more intense. This convinced us not only that we had to add to our cold and objective discourse the heat of subjectivity – ensuring that emotions too had plenty of room as we built up our arguments – but also that we had a lot to learn from the discoveries of the behavioural sciences when it came to denial, mourning, storytelling and all the other themes that could link psychological realities to collapse.

A gap has sometimes yawned between us and friends and colleagues who still clung to – and defended – an imaginary vision of continuity and linear progress. Over the years, we have clearly distanced ourselves from the *doxa*, that is to say the general opinion that gives a common meaning to the news of the world. Carry out the experiment for yourselves: listen to the news with this perspective in mind and you'll see the huge gap between *doxa* and reality. It's a strange feeling to be part of this world (more than ever), while being cut off from the dominant image that other people have of it. This often forces us to think about the relevance of our work. Have we gone crazy or become single-issue bores? Not necessarily. On the one hand, dialogue is always possible and, on the other, we cannot ignore the fact that we are far from being alone, as the number of collapsologists (which includes, strangely enough, many engineers and scientists) and other people sensitized to this theme is growing and turning into a self-aware movement, an ever denser and more interconnected network. In many countries, economic, scientific and military experts, as well as certain political movements (the degrowth movement, transition movement, Alternatiba, etc.), have no hesitation about openly discussing collapse scenarios. The worldwide blogosphere, although mainly English-speaking, is very active. In France, the Institut Momentum[8] has done pioneering work in this field, and we owe it a great deal. It is now difficult to ignore the coming collapse.

In the first part of this book, we will discuss the facts: what is it happening to our societies and to the Earth system? Are we really on the brink of disaster? Where is the most convincing evidence? We will see that it is the convergence of all 'crises' that makes this outcome possible. However, an overall collapse has not yet taken place (at least not in North Europe – Greece and Spain may be premonitory examples).

We must therefore tackle the perilous subject of futurology. So, in a second part, we will try to gather the evidence for this future. Finally, the third part will be an invitation to give concrete thickness to this notion of collapse. Why don't people believe in it? What do ancient civilizations teach us about it? How do people manage to live with it? How will we as a social body respond if this process lasts for dozens of years? What policies should we consider, not to avoid this eventuality but to get through it as 'humanely' as possible? Can we suffer a collapse in full awareness of what's happening? Is the situation so serious?

Part I

The Harbingers of Collapse

1

The Accelerating Vehicle

Take the metaphor of the car. At the beginning of the industrial era, the car suddenly appears. Only a few countries get in and drive off; they are then joined by others as the century proceeds. All the countries that have climbed on board – what we call industrial civilization – took a very particular route, one that we describe in this chapter. After a slow and gradual start, the car picks up speed at the end of the Second World War, and embarks on a breathtaking ascent called 'the great acceleration'.[1] Today, after some signs of overheating in the spluttering engine, the needle on the speedometer is starting to flicker. Will the needle continue to climb? Will it stabilize? Will it go back down?

A world of exponentials

Although we came across the idea at school, we are not accustomed to think in terms of 'exponential growth'. Of course, we can see a curve that goes up, indicating a growth. But what a growth it is! While the human mind can easily imagine arithmetical growth, for example a hair that grows one centimetre a month, it struggles to imagine exponential growth.

If you fold a large piece of cloth in half, after four folds its thickness will measure about 1 cm. If you could fold it in two another twenty-nine times, its thickness would have grown to 5,400 kilometres, the distance between Paris and Dubai. A few more folds would be enough to exceed the distance between the Earth and the Moon. A gross domestic product (GDP) (for example, China's) which is growing at 7 per cent a year represents an economic activity that doubles every ten years, and so quadruples in twenty years. After fifty years, we are dealing with a volume of 32 Chinese economies, i.e., at current values the equivalent of almost four additional world economies. Do you sincerely believe that this can be possible in the current state of our planet?

There are plenty of examples to describe the incredible behaviour of the exponential curve, from the water-lily equation, dear to Albert Jacquard,[2] to the chessboard on which each successive square is filled with twice the number of grains of rice as the previous one,[3] all showing the amazing and indeed counter-intuitive dynamic at work: when the effects of this growth become visible, it is often too late.

In mathematics, an exponential function goes all the way up to the sky. In the real world, on Earth, it hits a ceiling long before that. In ecology, this ceiling is called the capacity load of an ecosystem (denoted as K). There are usually three ways for a system to react to an exponential (see Figure 1.1). Take the classic example of an expanding population of rabbits in a meadow. Either the population gradually stabilizes before the ceiling, i.e., it does not grow any more, but finds a balance with its milieu (Figure 1.1a), or the population

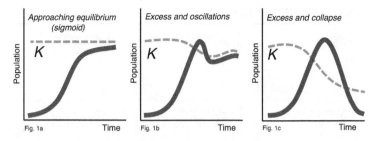

Figure 1.1 Reaction of a living system to exponential growth (the continuous curve represents a population and the dotted curve represents the carrying capacity of the milieu)

Source: after Meadows et al., 2004.

exceeds the maximum threshold that the meadow can support and then stabilizes in an oscillation that slightly damages the meadow (Figure 1.1b), or it breaks through the ceiling and continues to accelerate (overshooting), which leads to a collapse of the meadow, followed by that of the rabbit population (Figure 1.1c).[4]

These three theoretical diagrams can be used to illustrate three eras. So the first schema corresponds typically to the political ecology of the 1970s: we still had the time and opportunity to follow a path of 'sustainable development' (a 'steady-state economy'). The second represents the ecology of the 1990s when, thanks to the concept of ecological footprint, we realized that the *overall* carrying capacity of the Earth had been exceeded.[5] Since that period, every year, humankind as a whole has been 'consuming more than one planet' and ecosystems have become increasingly undermined. The last diagram represents the ecology of the 2010s: for the past twenty years, we have continued to accelerate *quite knowingly*, destroying the Earth system at an ever faster pace – the very system that welcomes and sustains us. Whatever the optimists may say, the time we are living is clearly marked by the spectre of a collapse.

SOCIO-ECONOMIC TRENDS

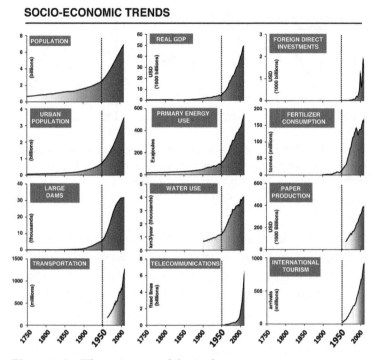

Figure 1.2a The trajectory of the Anthropocene: a summary

Source: after Will Steffen et al., 'The trajectory of the Anthropocene: The Great Acceleration', *The Anthropocene Review*, 2015: 1–18.

Total acceleration

We should by now realize that many of the parameters of our societies and of our impact on the planet are increasing at an exponential rate: population, GDP, water and energy consumption, the use of fertilizers, the production of engines and telephones, tourism, the atmospheric concentration of greenhouse gases, the number of floods, the damage to ecosystems, the destruction of forests, the extinction rate of species, and so on. The list is endless. This overall picture[7]

EARTH SYSTEM TRENDS

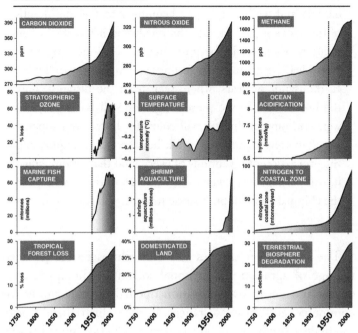

Figure 1.2b The trajectory of the Anthropocene: a summary

(see Figure 1.2a and 1.2b), very familiar to scientists, has almost become the logo of the new geological period called the Anthropocene, a time when humans have become a force that upsets the major biogeochemical cycles of the Earth system.

What has happened? Why this dramatic increase? Some Anthropocene specialists date the beginning of this period to the middle of the nineteenth century and the Industrial Revolution when the use of coal and steam became widespread, giving rise to the railway boom of the 1840s, followed by the discovery of the first oil deposits. As early as 1907, the philosopher Henri Bergson, with extraordinary prophetic insight, wrote:

A century has elapsed since the invention of the steam-engine, and we are only just beginning to feel the depths of the shock it gave us. But the revolution it has effected in industry has nevertheless upset human relations altogether. New ideas are arising, new feelings are on the way to flower. In thousands of years, when, seen from the distance, only the broad lines of the present age will still be visible, our wars and our revolutions will count for little, even supposing they are remembered at all; but the steam-engine, and the procession of inventions of every kind that accompanied it, will perhaps be spoken of as we speak of the bronze or of the chipped stone of prehistoric times: it will serve to define an age.[8]

The age of heat engines and the technosciences replaced the age of agrarian and artisanal societies. The appearance of fast and cheap transportation opened up new routes for commerce, and shrank distances. In the industrialized world, the hellish rhythms of automatized production lines became widespread and, gradually, *overall* material comfort levels increased. Decisive progress in public hygiene, food and medicine increased lifespan and reduced mortality rates considerably. World population, which had doubled about every thousand years over the last eight millennia, doubled in just one century. From one billion people in 1830, it grew to two billion in 1930. Then things really speeded up: in only forty years, the population doubled again. Four billion in 1970. Seven billion today. In the space of a single lifetime, a person born in the 1930s saw the population increase from two billion to seven billion! During the twentieth century, energy consumption increased tenfold, the extraction of industrial minerals by a factor of 27, and that of building materials by a factor of 34.[9] The scale and the speed of the changes we are triggering are unprecedented in history.

This huge acceleration can also be seen on the social level. The German philosopher and sociologist Hartmut Rosa describes three dimensions of this social acceleration.[10] The first is technical acceleration: 'the increase in travelling and communication speeds, indeed, lies behind that highly characteristic experience of our times, the "shrinking of space": distances in space appear to be shrinking as we can cross them more quickly and easily'.[11] The second is the acceleration in social change: our habits and our patterns of relationship are becoming transformed ever more quickly. For example, it is clear 'that our neighbours move in and then move out ever more frequently, that our life partners (or partners for parts of our lives), as well as our jobs, have ever shorter "half-lives", and that fashions, car models and musical styles succeed one another with increasing rapidity.' We are witnessing a veritable 'shrinking of the present'. The third acceleration is the acceleration in the rhythms of our lives: in reaction to technical and social acceleration, we try to live faster. We fill our timetables ever more efficiently; we strive to avoid 'wasting' this precious time and, strangely, the number of things we need (and want) to do seems to grow indefinitely. 'The acute "shortage of time" has become a permanent state of modern societies.'[12] The result? Happiness eludes us, we suffer burn-out, depression becomes endemic. And the height of progress is that this social acceleration that we relentlessly manufacture/suffer no longer aims to improve our standard of living, it just serves to maintain the status quo.

Where do the limits lie?

The essential question of our time is therefore to know where the ceiling is.[13] Do we have the capacity to continue to accelerate? Is there a limit (or several limits) to our exponential growth? And, if so, how long do we still have before things collapse?

It may be simple or even simplistic, but the metaphor of the car has the advantage of clearly distinguishing between the different 'problems' (call them 'crises') that we face. It suggests that there are two types of limit, or more precisely that there are *limits* on the one hand and *boundaries* on the other. The former cannot be crossed because they come up against the laws of thermodynamics: that's the problem of the fuel tank. The second *can* be crossed but they are no less insidious because they are invisible, and we realize that we are crossing them only when it is too late. This is the problem of speed and keeping the vehicle on course.

The *limits* of our civilization are imposed by the quantities of so-called 'stock' resources, which are by definition non-renewable (fossil fuels and ores), and 'flow' resources (water, wood, food, etc.): these are renewable but we are exhausting them far too quickly for them to have time to regenerate. However much the engine may gain in efficiency, there will always come a time when it can no longer work for lack of fuel (see chapter 2).

The *boundaries* of our civilization represent thresholds that cannot be crossed on pain of destabilizing and destroying the systems that keep it alive: for example, the climate, the major cycles of the Earth system, and ecosystems (which include all non-human living things). If the vehicle goes too fast, we can no longer perceive the details of the road, and this increases the risk of an accident (see chapter 3). We will try to see what happens when, without warning, the car leaves the route laid out and enters an uncertain and perilous world.

These crises are of profoundly different natures, but they all have the same common denominator: the car's acceleration. In addition, each of the limits and boundaries is *all by itself* capable of seriously destabilizing civilization. The problem, in our case, is that we are running up against several limits *simultaneously* and we have already crossed several boundaries!

As for the car itself, it has of course improved over the decades. It has become far more spacious, modern and comfortable, but at what a price! Not only is it impossible to slow down or turn – the accelerator pedal is glued to the floor and the steering wheel has got stuck (see chapter 4) – but, more embarrassingly, the driver's seat has become extremely fragile (see chapter 5).

The car is our society, our thermo-industrial civilization. We've climbed aboard and set off, our satnavs set for a sunny destination. No stop-offs are planned. Sitting comfortably in the passenger seat, we forget about speed, we ignore the living creatures we run over, the tremendous energy being expended and the amount of exhaust we are leaving behind us. As you well know, once you're on the motorway, all that matters is the arrival time, the temperature of the air conditioning and the quality of the radio programme … .

2

When the Engine Dies
(Limits that Cannot be Crossed)

Let's start with energy. This is often considered as a secondary technical issue after the main priorities, namely employment, the economy and democracy. Now energy is at the heart of every civilization, especially our own industrial and consumerist civilization. You can sometimes do without creativity, purchasing power or investment capacity, but you can't do without energy. It's a physical principle: without energy, there is no movement. Without fossil fuels, globalization, industry and economic activity as we know them are finished.

Over the last century, oil has become essential as the main fuel for modern transport, and thus for global trade, the construction and maintenance of infrastructure, the mining of resources, logging, fishing and agriculture. It has an exceptional energy density, is easy to transport and store, and simple to use: it fuels 95 per cent of transport.

A society that has taken the path of exponential growth needs the production and consumption of energy to follow

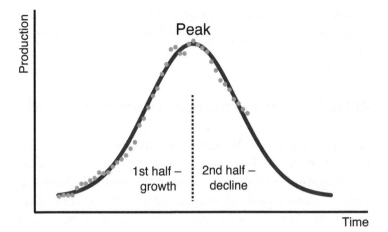

Figure 2.1 The concept of 'peak' was introduced by geophysicist Marion King Hubbert in 1956 for conventional oil production in the United States

Note: The grey dots that follow the curve represent Norwegian oil production which peaked in 2001.

Source: BP Stat. Review, 2013.

this same path. In other words, to maintain our civilization in working order, we must constantly *increase* our energy consumption and production. But we have reached a peak.

A peak is the moment when the extraction rate of a resource reaches an upper limit before declining inexorably. This is more than a theory, it's a kind of geological principle: to begin with, extractable resources are easy to access; production explodes, then stagnates and finally declines when the only raw material left is not easy to access, thus describing a bell curve (see Figure 2.1). The top of the curve, the peak moment, does not mean the resource has been depleted but rather signals the beginning of its decline. This notion is conventionally used for extractable resources, such as fossil fuels or ores (phosphorus, uranium, metals, etc.), but it is also applied (sometimes wrongly) to other aspects of society, as well as to the population or to GDP, in so far as these parameters are strongly correlated with the extraction of resources.

At the top of the peak, does energy starts to fall?

But we have reached the top of the curve of conventional oil production. As the International Energy Agency, known for its optimism about oil reserves, has itself admitted, the global peak in conventional oil, accounting for 80 per cent of oil production, was crossed in 2006.[1] We have since been on a 'wavy plateau'. Past this plateau, world oil production will begin to decline.[2]

According to the most recent statistics,[3] half of the twenty leading producing countries, representing more than three-quarters of the world's oil production, have already crossed their peak, including the United States, Russia, Iran, Iraq, Venezuela, Mexico, Norway, Algeria and Libya.[4] In the 1960s, for every barrel consumed, the industry discovered six new ones. Today, *with an ever more efficient technology*, the world consumes seven barrels for each barrel discovered.

In a scientific overview published in 2012,[5] British researchers concluded that 'more than two-thirds of current crude oil production capacity will need to be replaced by 2030, simply to keep production constant. Given the long-term decline in new discoveries, this will present a major challenge even if "above-ground" [technical and economic] conditions prove favourable.'[6] So, in the next fifteen years, *in order to maintain itself*, the industry will need a supply of 60 million barrels per day, equivalent to the daily capacity of six Saudi Arabias.

The state of oil reserves is becoming clearer, and a growing number of multinationals, governments, experts and international organizations are increasingly pessimistic as to the future of production. The authors of the aforementioned study conclude, 'On the basis of current evidence we suggest that a peak of conventional oil production before 2030 appears likely and there is a significant risk of a peak before 2020', a conclusion shared by reports financed by the British government,[7] and the US[8] and German[9] armies. In short, there is a growing consensus about the fact that the age of easily accessible oil is over and we are entering a new era.[10]

The oil situation is so tense that many business executives are sounding the alarm. In Great Britain, a consortium of large companies, known as ITPOES (the UK Industry Taskforce on Peak Oil and Energy Security), wrote in its February 2010 report, 'As we reach maximum oil extraction rates [...] [w]e must plan for a world in which oil prices are likely to be both higher and more volatile and where oil price shocks have the potential to destabilise economic, political and social activity.'[11]

For more optimistic observers, on the contrary, estimates concluding that a 'peak' has been reached are based on maximum extractable quantities that are far too alarmist. So a group of researchers has looked into the matter, comparing a range of scenarios from the most optimistic to the most pessimistic. The result was that only the scenarios considered to be pessimistic fit the actual data observed over the last eleven years.[12] The study thus confirmed that the worldwide production of conventional oil has entered an irreversible decline.

Fine: but what about new deposits, in particular so-called unconventional forms of oil, i.e., heavy hydrocarbons and/or hydrocarbons trapped at great depths between the sand, the tar and the rocks of the Earth's crust? Won't the offshore platforms in the depths near the Brazilian and Arctic coasts, the oil sands of Canada, and shale gas and oil gradually replace conventional crude?

No. And the facts are overwhelming. In regard to shale oil and gas, let's just pass over the fact that extraction techniques threaten the environment and the health of local residents,[13] cause micro-earthquakes,[14] leakages of methane[15] and radioactive material,[16] consume a lot of energy (we will come back to this),[17] sand and fresh water,[18] and contaminate the groundwater tables.[19]

In fact, drilling companies in this domain mostly produce dreadful financial results. According to a report from the American energy department, the combined assets of 127 companies that drill for shale oil and gas in the United States show a deficit of 106 billion dollars for the fiscal year 2013–14,[20] a deficit which they have hastened to fill by opening up new credit lines. But to attract more investment and show financial analysts a positive result, they have had to sell 73 billion dollars' worth of assets. The result has been exploding debts and an increasing lack of capacity to generate the revenue necessary to repay them.[21]

A study commissioned by the British government warns, 'Greater dependency on resources using hydraulic fracturing will aggravate the tendency to increase average decline rates, since wells have no plateau and decline extremely quickly, sometimes 90 per cent or more during the five first years.'[22] Others say the figure is a 60 per cent decline in production in the first year alone.[23] So, to avoid bankruptcy, companies must drill ever more wells and pile up ever more debt, both to offset the decline of wells already worked and to continue to increase the production that will serve to repay their growing debts. This is a race against the clock whose outcome is already known.

It's this little bubble that many people did not see (or refused to see) when they trumpeted that these unconventional fossil fuels would enable the United States to regain a certain energy independence.[24] In an attempt to artificially inflate the growth and competitiveness of the United States, the Federal Reserve Bank allowed oil companies to borrow at extremely low interest rates, thereby manufacturing a time bomb: the slightest rise in interest rates would push the most fragile companies to the edge of bankruptcy. The problem is pretty much the same for shale gas.[25] The Obama administration thought that the whole edifice would stand for only a few years after reaching its ceiling in 2016.[26]

Estimates – very optimistic estimates – from the International Energy Agency indicate that the oil sands of Canada and Venezuela will each provide five million barrels per day in 2030, which represents less than 6 per cent of total fuel production by this date (projected).[27] So, *even in the best-case scenario*, it is impossible to compensate for the decline of conventional fuels in this way.

What about the Arctic? Risks to the environment[28] and risks for investors[29] are far too significant here. Major oil companies withdrew from the race *even when the price per barrel was raised*: they included Shell, which suspended its explorations in 2013,[30] and Total which did the same, warning all those active in the sector of the potential dangers.[31]

Biofuels are hardly any more 'reassuring'. Their contribution is forecast to be limited to 5 per cent of the fuel supply for the next ten to fifteen years,[32] not to mention the fact that some pose a serious threat to food security in many countries.[33]

It is hardly realistic to imagine that electrifying the transport system will replace oil. Electric networks, batteries and spare parts are manufactured from rare metals and other raw materials (which are running out), and the entire electric system consumes fossil fuels: they are needed for the transport of spare parts, workers and materials, for the construction and maintenance of power stations and for the extraction of ores. Without oil, the current electric system, including nuclear power, will collapse.

In fact, it is unimaginable that we could replace oil with the other fuels we are familiar with. On the one hand, not natural gas, nor coal, nor wood, nor uranium possess the exceptional qualities of oil, which is easy to transport and very dense in energy. On the other hand, these energies would be exhausted in no time at all, not only because the date of their peak is approaching[34] but also and mainly because most of the machines and infrastructure necessary for their operation need oil. The decline in oil will therefore lead to the decline of all other forms of energy. It is thus dangerous to underestimate the magnitude of the task that faces us if we are to compensate for the decline in conventional oil.

But that's not all. The main ores and metals are following the same path as energy, moving towards a peak.[35] A recent study has assessed the scarcity of 88 non-renewable resources and the probability that there will be a permanent shortage of them by 2030.[36] Those for which this is a high probability include silver, essential to the manufacture of wind turbines, indium, an essential component for several photovoltaic cells, and lithium, used in batteries. And the study concludes that these shortages will have a devastating impact on our way of life. In the same vein, we have recently seen estimates in which peaks will be reached for phosphorus[37] (an essential fertilizer in industrial agriculture), fisheries[38] and even drinking water.[39] And the list could easily be extended. As the specialist in mineral resources Philippe Bihouix explains in *L'Âge des low tech* (*The Age of Low Tech*),

> we could allow ourselves a degree of latitude when it comes to any of these resources, energy or metals. But the challenge

now is that we are having to face them all at pretty much the same time: [there is] no more of the energy needed for the less concentrated metals, [there are] no more of the metals needed for less accessible energy.[40]

So we are rapidly approaching what Richard Heinberg calls 'peak everything'.[41] Remember the surprising fact about exponentials: once the consequences are visible, it's all just a matter of years, or even months.

In short, we can expect an imminent decline in the availability of fossil fuels and the raw materials that drive industrial civilization. For now, no alternative seems likely to make up for the coming scarcity. The fact that production is stagnating at the expense of increasingly intense prospecting on the part of oil majors with ever more efficient technologies is all too clear a sign. Since 2000, investments made by the industry have grown on average by 10.9 per cent a year, ten times faster than in the previous decade.[42] The very fact that oil sands, shale oil, biofuels, solar panels and wind turbines are now being taken seriously by those same industries that formerly looked down on them indicates that we are moving into a new era – the era of the peak.

But what comes after the peak? A slow, gradual decline in the production of fossil fuels? Possibly, but there are two reasons for doubting this. The first is that, once they are past the peak of *their own deposits*, oil-producing countries will have to deal with growing domestic consumption. If they decide – legitimately – to stop exporting in order to meet this demand, it will be to the detriment of the major importing countries (including France), and this could trigger predatory wars that will disrupt the productive capacity of oil-producing countries. In any case, the decline will probably be faster than expected. And the second reason for doubt is that ...

At the top of the peak, there is a wall!

Normally, after climbing a bell curve on one side, there is
the other side to go down. It would be logical to believe that
this still leaves half of the oil we discovered under the Earth's
surface. True! And it's a proven fact: the quantities of fossil
fuel stocked underground – and proven to exist – are still
gigantic and all the more significant if we take into account
the methane hydrates that we might imagine drawing on
after the melting of the Siberian and Canadian permafrost.
So is this good news?

Let's not rejoice too soon. First, it would be a disaster
for the climate (see next chapter). Also, even if we wanted,
we would never be able to extract all that oil. The reason is
simple: to extract oil, it takes energy, a lot of energy – for
prospecting, feasibility studies, machinery, wells, pipelines,
roads, and for the maintenance and the security of all these
infrastructures, and so on. Now common sense dictates
that in extraction, the amount of energy garnered should
be greater than the energy invested. Logical enough. If you
garner less than you invest, it's not worth digging. This rela-
tion between the energy produced and the energy invested is
called the energy return on investment (EROI).

This is an absolutely crucial point. After the effort
expended in an extraction, it is the *energy surplus* which allows
a civilization to develop. At the beginning of the twentieth
century, US oil had a fantastic EROI of 100:1 (for one unit
of energy invested, one hundred units were recovered). You
hardly needed to start digging before the oil started gushing.
In 1990, it had fallen to only 35:1, and today it is about 11:1.[43]
As a comparison, the average EROI of the world production
of conventional oil is between 10:1 and 20:1.[44] In the United
States, the EROI for oil sands lies between 2:1 and 4:1, that

for agrofuels between 1:1 and 1.6:1 (10:1 in the case of etha-
nol made from cane sugar), and for nuclear power between
5:1 and 15:1.[45] The EROI for coal is about 50:1 (in China,
27:1), for shale oil about 5:1 and for natural gas about 10:1.[46]
All these EROIs are not only declining, but declining *at an
accelerating rate* since it is always necessary to dig deeper and
deeper, go further out to sea and use ever more expensive
techniques and infrastructures so as to maintain the level of
production. Think, for example, of the energy that would be
needed to inject thousands of tons of CO_2 or fresh water into
ageing deposits, and the roads that would need to be built,
and the kilometres that would have to be covered in order to
reach the remote areas of Siberia …

The EROI concept does not only apply to fossil fuel. To
obtain energy from wind turbines for example, first you have
to spend energy to gather all the raw materials used in their
manufacture, and then to manufacture them, install them
and maintain them. In the United States, concentrated solar
power (those big mirrors in the desert) produces a yield of
around 1.6:1. Photovoltaics in Spain produce around 2.5:1.[47]
As for wind power, it initially seems to offer a better yield of
about 18:1.[48] Sadly, these figures do not take into account
the intermittent nature of this type of energy and the need to
back it up with a storage system or thermal power plant. If
we take this into account, the EROI for wind turbines comes
down to 3.8:1.[49] Only hydroelectricity apparently offers
a comfortable yield of between 35:1 and 49:1. But besides
the fact that this type of production seriously disrupts natural habitats,[50] a recent study has shown that 3,700 projects
underway or planned across the world would increase global
electricity production by only 2 per cent (from 16 per cent
to 18 per cent).[51]

In short, renewable energy does not have the potential
to offset the decline in fossil fuel, and there are not enough

fossil fuels (or ores) to massively develop renewable energies so as to offset the predicted decline in fossil fuels. As Gail Tverberg, actuary and specialist in the economics of energy, puts it, 'We are being told, "Renewables will save us," but this is basically a lie. Wind and solar PV are just as much a part of our current fossil fuel system as any other source of electricity.'[52]

The problem is that our modern societies need a minimum EROI to maintain all the services currently offered to the population.[53] The principle of energy use is roughly the following: we first allocate all the energy surplus we have to the tasks essential for our survival, such as food production, building and heating our habitats, making our clothes, and running health systems in the cities. Then we split the remaining balance between the systems of justice, national security, defence, social security, health and education. Finally, if we have any energy surplus left, we use it for our entertainment (tourism, cinema, etc.).

Today, the minimum EROI to provide all of these services has been assessed as within a range of between 12:1 and 13:1.[54] In other words, there is a threshold beneath which we should not venture unless we are prepared to decide collectively – and with all the difficulties that this implies – which services are to be maintained and which it will be necessary to give up.[55] With an average EROI in decline for fossil fuels, and an EROI of no more than 12:1 for the majority of renewable energies, we are coming dangerously close to this threshold.

Of course, all these ranges of numbers can be argued with, and some people will not fail to question them, but the general principle is less controversial. The idea we need to grasp is that we are facing a thermodynamic wall that is getting *ever more rapidly closer*. Today, each unit of energy is extracted at an ever higher environmental, economic and energy cost.

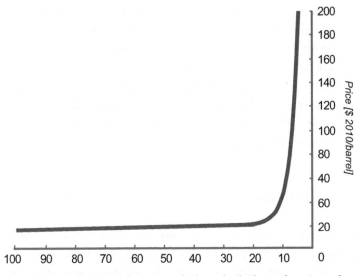

Figure 2.2 Modelling the price of a barrel of oil as a function of the EROI (using the historical correlations observed)

Source: after K. Heun and M. De Wit, 'Energy return on (energy) invested (EROI), oil prices, and energy transitions', *Energy Policy* 40, 2012: 147–58.

Economic indices also make it possible to visualize this wall. Two research teams on different methods have recently modelled the complex relationship between EROI and production costs (price per barrel).[56] Their conclusions are the same: when the EROI of fossil fuel dips below 10:1, prices rise in a non-linear way, in other words, exponentially (see Figure 2.2). This upward trend in production costs is also noticeable for gas, coal and uranium, as well as for metals and ores indispensable for the production of renewable energy.[57]

Knowing that about two-thirds of the growth in the years 1945–75 was due to the burning of fossil fuels – the remainder being the product of labour and investment[58] – we can deduce that the inexorable decline of the EROI for fossil fuel will result in a huge shortfall that will make it impossible to keep the promise of economic growth.[59] In other words, an energy decline is the sign of nothing less than the definitive end of global economic growth.

A glance at the curve in Figure 2.2 will also help us to realize that we are really dealing with a wall, to use the metaphor of the car. This wall is an impassable wall as it is built on the laws of thermodynamics.

And before the wall ... a precipice

In these conditions, it is hard to see how our civilization could rediscover the prospect of abundance or at least of continuity. But, as surprising as it may appear, the energy shortage is not the most urgent threat to our engine. Something else threatens to bring it to a halt just before that point: the financial system.

In reality, the energy system and the financial system are closely linked, and the one cannot function without the other. They form a sort of belt drive, an energy–financial axis, which represents the heart of our industrial civilization. We can become aware of this link by observing the close correlation between GDP and the oil production curve (see Figure 2.3). A recession means a high oil price and low consumption; a period of expansion indicates the opposite, a low oil price and high consumption. This mechanism is not a simple correlation but a causal relationship: a historical study has shown that, out of eleven recessions that took place during the twentieth century, ten were preceded by a sharp increase in oil prices (see Figure 2.4).[60] In other words, an energy crisis precedes a serious economic crisis. This was the case during the oil shocks of the 1970s and during the 2008 crisis.

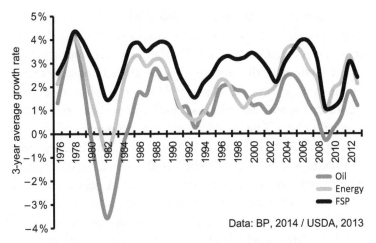

Figure 2.3 Growth rate of oil, energy and global GDP

Source: after Gail E. Tverberg, 'Energy and the Economy – Twelve Basic Principles,' *Our Finite World*, 14 August 2014.

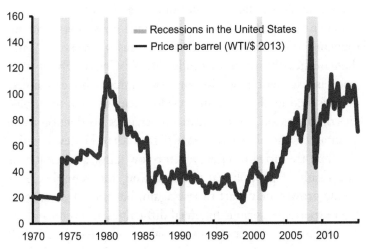

Figure 2.4 Price of a barrel of oil and periods of recession

Source: after J. Hamilton, 'Causes and Consequences of the Oil Shock of 2007–08', National Bureau of Economic Research, 2009 (updated by the authors).

To consider economic problems while forgetting their origins in the energy situation is a serious mistake. But the opposite is equally true. Gail Tverberg has become an expert in the analysis of this energy–finance axis and observes that, in the context of a peak, it is no longer possible to extract significant quantities of fossil fuel without incurring ever greater debts. 'The problem we are encountering now is that once resource costs get too high, the debt-based system no longer works. A new debt-based financial system likely won't work any better than the old one'.[61] A debt system has a bulimic need for growth and thus energy. But the opposite is also true: our energy system 'shoots up' on debts. Thus the belt drive works both ways: a decline in oil production pushes our economies towards recession; conversely, economic recessions accelerate the decline in energy production.[62] More specifically, the global economic system is now caught between a high price and a low price of oil. But these two extremes are the two sides of the same coin.

When the price of oil is too high, consumers end up reducing their expenditure, which causes recessions (and then pushes the price of crude down). Conversely, a high price is excellent news for oil companies, who can invest in prospecting through the development of new technologies of extraction, which ultimately enables production to be maintained and alternative energy sources to be developed.

When the price of energy is too low (after a recession or as a result of geopolitical manipulation, for example), economic growth may start to rise again, but the oil companies then experience serious financial difficulties and reduce their investments (as we saw from the fall in oil prices in 2014),[63] which dangerously compromises future production. The 2014 report of the International Energy Agency[64] observes that the effort required to offset the natural decline of old deposits which have come to maturity 'appears all the more difficult to keep up now that the price of a barrel has fallen to 80 dollars, [...] especially for oil sands and ultra-deep drilling off the coasts of Brazil'. And the Agency's chief economist, the very optimistic Fatih Birol, notes that 'clouds are starting to gather on the long-term horizon of production of global oil production; they may be bringing stormy conditions our way'.[65]

The fragility of the global financial system no longer needs to be demonstrated. It consists of a complex network of monies outstanding and bonds, linking together the balance sheets of countless intermediaries such as banks, hedge funds and insurers. As demonstrated by the bankruptcy of Lehman Brothers and its aftermath in 2008, these inter-dependencies have created an environment conducive to knock-on or contagion effects[66] (see chapter 5). Moreover, the global political and financial oligarchy shows no sign that it has actually understood the diagnosis; it thrashes about making inappropriate decisions, thus contributing to the further weakening of this economic system. The most urgent limiting factor for the future of oil production, then, is not the quantity of remaining reserves or the energy return rate (EROI), as many people think, but 'how long our current networked economic system can hold together'.[67]

In short, our economies are doomed to try and maintain a very precarious and oscillating balance, a roller-coaster ride, based on the price of a barrel of oil being between about US$80 and US$130 a barrel, while hoping and praying that the now extremely volatile financial system does not collapse. In fact, a period of low economic growth or recession could reduce available credit and investment on the part of oil companies and could cause the engine to seize up even before the physical extraction limit is reached.

Without a functioning economy, easily accessible energy ceases to be available. And without accessible energy, it's the end of the economy as we know it: swift transport, long and fluid supply chains, industrial agriculture, heating, water purification, the internet, and so on. But history shows us that societies are quickly destabilized when tummies start to rumble. During the economic crisis of 2008, the dramatic increase in food prices provoked food riots in no fewer than thirty-five countries.[68]

In his latest book, the former petroleum geologist and energy advisor to the British government, Jeremy Leggett, identified five global systemic risks linked directly to energy and threatening the stability of the global economy: oil depletion, carbon emissions, the financial value of fossil fuel reserves, shale gas, and the financial sector. 'A market shock involving any of these would be capable of triggering a tsunami of economic and social problems, and, of course, there is no law of economics that says only one can hit at one time'.[69] So we are probably listening to the last splutterings of the engine of our industrial civilization before it dies.

3

Leaving the Road
(Boundaries that Can be Crossed)

In addition to the impassable limits that physically prevent any economic system from growing unstoppably, there are invisible, unclear 'boundaries' that are difficult to predict. These are thresholds beyond which the systems on which we depend get out of hand, such as the climate, ecosystems and the major biogeochemical cycles of the planet. It is possible to cross these thresholds, but the consequences are just as catastrophic. Here, then, the metaphor of the wall is not very useful. Boundaries would be more adequately represented by the edges of the road beyond which the car leaves an area of stability and faces unpredictable obstacles.

As yet, we are not fully aware of the consequences of crossing these 'boundaries'. Thus, unlike limits, which stop the car in its tracks, boundaries do not prevent us from causing disasters; they leave us free and responsible for our choices, *obliged* solely by our ethics and our ability to predict disasters. We cannot create energy from nothing, but we can choose to live in a climate with a temperature of +4°C above the historical average (which is what we are doing in any case). However, to make responsible choices, you need to know the consequences of your actions. But most often, these are known only *after* exceeding these thresholds, when it's already too late.

Global heating and cold sweats

The climate is the best known of these invisible boundaries and over the years it has acquired a special status. Indeed, according to some experts, the consequences of global heating have the power *on their own* to cause global, massive and brutal disasters that could lead to the end of civilization or even of the human species. At the beginning of 2014, we were provided with an extraordinary scientific overview, the fifth IPCC report, which was now categorical in its conclusions: the climate is heating up because of the emission of greenhouse gases produced by human activity.[1] The average global temperature has increased by 0.85°C since 1880, and the trend accelerated over a period of sixty years. This latest report confirms the 'rule' that the most alarming predictions of previous reports become realities.[2] So we are emerging from the conditions required to limit heating to an average of +2°C in 2050, and we could reach +4.8°C by 2100 compared to the period 1986–2005. Note in passing that the initial projections of the IPCC on global temperature have been remarkably accurate until now.[3]

Disasters are not just about future generations; they concern present generations. Rising temperatures are *already causing* longer and more intense heatwaves and extreme events (storms, hurricanes, floods, droughts, etc.) that have caused significant damage in the last decade,[4] such as that suffered by Europe in 2003 (which caused the death of

70,000 people[5] and cost the European agricultural industry 13 billion euros) and, more recently, by Russia, Australia and the United States.[6] In 2010, the episodes of drought in Russia, for example, lopped 25 per cent off production in the agricultural sector and 15 billion dollars off the economy (1 per cent of GDP), forcing the government to abandon any export plans for that year.[7]

There are *already* water shortages in densely populated areas,[8] economic losses, social unrest and political instability,[9] the spread of contagious diseases,[10] the spread of bugs and pests,[11] the extinction of many living species (see the next section), irreversible and serious damage to unique ecosystems,[12] melting polar ice and glaciers,[13] as well as decreases in agricultural yields. So much for the present.

In *Climate Wars*, military specialist Gwynne Dyer describes the geopolitical consequences that could be provoked by global heating of a few degrees. Drawing on the conclusions of reports written by former senior military officials in the US government, as well as many interviews with experts, Dyer covers a number of scenarios ranging from a world temperature +2°C above average, already catastrophic, to 'annihilation' at +9°C.

In a world with an average of +2°C, there will be a considerable risk of war. India, for example, has already decided to build a barrier two and a half metres high along the three thousand kilometres of its border with Bangladesh, one of the countries from which a very large number of refugees could arrive due to the sea flooding its low coastal regions.[14] In the rest of the world, massive droughts, recurring hurricanes and population displacements would put a huge strain on the boundaries between rich and poor. Rich countries would be destabilized by severe agricultural problems, and some islands in the Indian Ocean would need to be evacuated. That is a quick overview of the scenario at +2°C, which we will not dwell on, as it is not even on the agenda any-more! Indeed, Dyer's book is based on reports prior to 2008, and in particular on the IPCC 2007 report, which itself syn-thesizes scientific work published before 2002.

In November 2012, the World Bank published a report[15] that it had commissioned from a team of climatologists at the University of Potsdam on the consequences of an increase of +4°C on our societies and on life on Earth. An average of +4°C means increases of up to +10°C on the continents (we need to imagine, for example, a summer at an average of +8°C in the south of France!). The sea level would rise by about one metre in 2100 (confirmed by the new IPCC report), threatening the main cities of Mozambique, Madagascar, Mexico, Venezuela, India, Bangladesh, Indonesia, the Philippines and Vietnam, and rendering the main deltas use-less for agriculture (Bangladesh, Egypt, Vietnam and West Africa). The report makes for grim reading, and the conse-quences it describes are particularly catastrophic; they clearly threaten the very possibility of maintaining our civilization in its present shape.

The serious economic and demographic crises that European societies underwent before the industrial era are all related to climate disruptions. A study published in 2011 goes even further, analysing the waves of causal chains that, between 1500 and 1800, linked climate change to major agricultural, socio-economic and demographic disasters (see Figure 3.1).[16] In fact, while economic downturns were the *direct* causes of the serious social crises that triggered demo-graphic collapse, the climate has always been the root cause. And at the heart of the process, we always find food shortages.

We now know that global heating causes and will cause serious water-supply problems and declines in agricultural yield (the two are not always linked). At +2°C, the number of people faced with severe water shortages could increase by

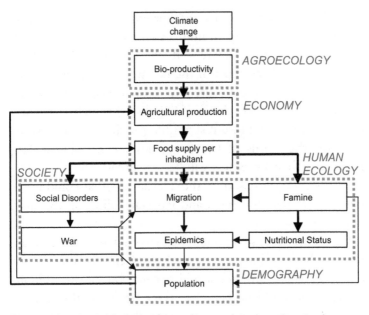

Figure 3.1 Causal links between climate change and major human crises in pre-industrial Europe. The thickness of the arrow indicates the strength of the correlation

Source: after D. D. Zhang et al., 'The causality analysis of climate change and large-scale human crisis', *PNAS* 108(42), 2011: 17296–301.

15 per cent.[17] Since 1980, global maize and wheat production have fallen by 3.8 per cent and 5.5 per cent respectively, compared to a simulation where there is no climate change.[18] Globally, wheat yields have tended to stagnate over the last twenty years, despite considerable technical progress.[19] In the north of Europe, Russia and Canada, precipitation will be more intense and winters warmer,[20] which points to better yields and new arable land. But the flood risk will also be higher.[21] Conversely, in other regions, researchers expect more frequent water shortages and extreme weather events (heat, drought and storms),[22] which will lower overall agricultural production.

With +2°C, Indian agricultural production would decrease by 25 per cent, causing an unprecedented famine: 'but [this] does not begin to compare with the plight of Bangladesh, where the southern third of the country – home to 60 million people – would be literally disappearing beneath the waves due to sea-level rise.'[23] If Bangladeshis realize that and decide to look for those responsible for this 'climatic genocide' (in the words of the Bangladeshi climatologist Atiq Rahman), 'their bitterness will be very great'.[24] With a chilling realism, Dyer describes the nuclear war that could break out in 2036 between India and Pakistan following this kind of conflict.

Geopolitical tensions would be exacerbated by the increasing number of climate refugees.[25] In Central America, for example, where drought would become the norm, millions of refugees would be halted in their tracks by the frontier with the United States – a frontier that is becoming ever more impermeable. The same social and humanitarian disaster could take place in southern Europe, given the influx of refugees from Africa, the Near East and the Middle East.

Episodes of increased drought can also lead to a fall in the electricity production of thermal and nuclear power plants,[26] which further weakens the ability of people to adapt and survive the consequences of global heating, especially in cities.

One of the biggest risks of climate change is that of growing inequalities (see chapter 8). As Leon Fuerth, a former US national security advisor during Al Gore's time as vice president and one of the authors of the report 'The Age of Consequences' puts it, even the richest countries 'will be forced to engage in long, nightmarish episodes of triage: deciding what and who can be salvaged from engulfment by a disordered environment'.[27] As for the fate of the most deprived, 'We have already previewed the images, in the course of the organizational and spiritual unravelling that was Hurricane Katrina.'[28]

Today, we find ourselves in ideal conditions for reaching a global agreement on the climate since none of the world's great powers has felt under attack since the end of the Cold War. But 'the deeper we get into the food shortages attendant on global heating, the more difficult it will be to make international deals of any kind'.[29]

The latest IPCC report indicates the possibility of a 'breakdown in food systems' which will aggravate pre-existing situations of poverty and famine (particularly in cities) and increase 'the risks of violent conflict in the form of civil wars and violence between groups'. But the problem with this monumental report is that it does not take into account the amplifying effects of many climate feedback loops, such as the release of large quantities of methane due to the thawing of the permafrost (hence the recurring optimism of the different versions of these reports). Now, these loops are likely to be triggered once we reach +3°C or +4°C. Thus, beyond a temperature increase of this kind, it is very difficult to describe precisely what could happen. However, the scenarios depicted by the experts are generally unanimous and point to looming disasters.

We can get an idea of the magnitude of the *imaginable* changes by noting that, when the atmosphere of the last 100 million years contained levels of CO_2 that we could reach at the end of the century, the average temperature of the planet was 16°C higher than it is today.[30] Conversely, 10,000 years ago, and with temperatures 5°C lower, the Earth was plunged into an ice age, the ocean level was 120 metres lower than today and a layer of ice hundreds of metres thick covered northern Europe.

According to James Lovelock, if the CO_2 level reaches 500 ppm or more (we reached 400 ppm on 9 May 2013), most of the Earth's surface will turn into desert and bush, leaving a remnant of civilization – just a few million people in the Arctic Basin and Greenland.

> The Earth has recovered from fevers like this [in the past] [...] but if we continue business as usual, our species may never again enjoy the lush and verdant world we had only a hundred years ago. What is most in danger is civilization; humans are tough enough for breeding pairs to survive, and [...] in spite of the heat there will still be places on Earth that are pleasant enough by our standards; the survival of plants through the Eocene confirm it. [...] But if these huge changes do occur it seems likely that few of the teeming billions now alive will survive.[31]

Dyer, worried about such a scenario, asked climatologists if they found that possible, and almost all among them did not find it excessive.

That is what might happen if we do not reach an international agreement on climate change and if we continue to burn fossil fuels for a few more years. For we must not forget that even if we stopped emitting greenhouse gases *completely and immediately*, the climate would continue to heat up for several decades. It would take several centuries or even millennia to return to anything like the conditions of pre-industrial climate stability found in the Holocene.

If, by magic, we could extract and burn all the remaining fossil fuels – and the proven reserves are huge – the problems would be much more serious than those we have described above. In the fifth IPCC report, the worst-case scenario indicates an increase of between +8°C and +12°C for 2300. But in 2013, the famous climate scientist James Hansen and his team calculated the trajectory of a scenario in which we would manage to burn one-third of the proven reserves at the current rate, i.e., in less than a century. It would lead us to an average global temperature of +16°C, in other words +30°C at the poles and +20°C on the continents.[32] At this temperature, the world would become uninhabitable for most living beings, and even human perspiration would not be enough to maintain our bodies at 37°C. But don't worry: as we have seen in the previous chapter, we won't manage to burn all that oil ...

In fact, this scenario is unrealistic: well before it happens, the circulation of ocean currents could change, as it has done in the past, creating a risk of anoxia (lack of oxygen) in the depths of the ocean. If the anoxic layer reaches the surface of the oceans, where the light enters, we would then witness the proliferation of bacteria producing hydrogen sulphide, a gas known to destroy the ozone layer and make the atmosphere unbreathable. These 'Canfield Oceans', which have occurred on Earth in the past, would annihilate most marine and terrestrial life. Although this is only a hypothesis for the moment, it is still taken very seriously by some scientists. According to Dennis Bushnell, director of research at NASA, it is even conceivable that this might happen before 2100.

All these facts, these figures, these hypotheses, these projections and what our imagination can do with them point to what Chris Rapley, former director of the British Antarctic Survey, calls climate 'monsters'.

Who will kill the last animal on the planet?

Let's not exaggerate things – but still, it must be recognized that, over the past few years, humans have been quite effective in eradicating other living things. And the 'loss of biodiversity' is not a trivial phenomenon. It involves the destruction of many territories, in which billions of plants, animals, fungi and micro-organisms live and interact, and quite simply the disappearance of these living beings. But we human beings depend for our survival on these beings, on our interactions with them and *on the interactions that take place between them.*

Of course, species extinctions are natural phenomena, just like the appearance of new species. But the problem is that the rate of disappearance has shot up. A recent estimate shows that it is today at least a thousand times higher than the geological average as exemplified by fossils[33] and that it is increasing constantly and dramatically. According to the latest surveys, the state of biodiversity continues to worsen,[34] despite the *increasing* efforts we are deploying to protect and conserve it.[35] All the tremendous efforts that human beings are making to protect other living beings from their destructive power are still not enough.[36]

Very recently, a series of disturbing studies has darkened the picture even more, highlighting the extinction of *ecological interactions.* When a species dies, it never dies alone: it usually takes some of its neighbours with it without anyone noticing. Extinctions are like shocks that spread across the food web, affecting predators and prey of the 'endangered' species (vertically) and impacting indirectly on other species indirectly related to the latter (horizontally).[37] For example, the extermination of sea otters causes a proliferation of sea urchins (their prey), which transforms the seabed into deserts, which in turn impacts on other food chains and other predators.

The living world is not simply woven from a web of predation, and the shock wave can also spread through the parallel – and very rich – networks of mutual dependencies, like seed dispersal or pollination. Allowing a species to die out deprives others of valuable and even vital resources. We are discovering, for example, that the collapse of the populations of some pollinators can cause the widespread collapse of all the pollinators of an ecosystem and thus have a serious impact on the plants that depend on it, i.e., the agricultural yields.[38] It therefore affects not only human populations that feed on these ecosystems but also all the animals that depend on these plants which have nothing to do with the pollinators in question.

The consequences of the extinction of species may even modify the physical characteristics of the milieu. For example, the disappearance of bird species in New Zealand significantly decreases the pollination of the shrub *Rhabdothamnus solandri*; this reduces the density of its population,[39] and therefore affects soil, climate and the temperature and humidity of the ecosystem.

But there are even worse consequences. The shock wave can also strike us with unexpected speed. A study published in 2013 showed that the disappearance of ecological interactions ('functional extinctions') *precedes* the extinctions of populations. In other words, a species (the otter, for example) is already losing 'connections' with its neighbours *as soon as decline sets in*, entailing the disappearance (in 80 per cent of cases) of other species around it well before it has died out itself. These indirect and silent extinctions can begin very early, even before the population of the endangered species has lost a third of its total population (whereas it is not officially declared an endangered species until its decline has reached a figure of 30 per cent). After this point – paradoxically – the most endangered species are not the ones we imagine but those that are *indirectly related to those we think are most endangered*. Even ecologists, long aware of these effects, have been surprised by the extent of such 'domino effects'. What are now known as co-extinctions are potentially the most numerous,[40] but they are unpredictable, and we do not observe them until it's too late. That is one possible explanation for the catastrophic extent of the destruction of biodiversity through human activity.

What is the result? We have already entered a silent spring.[41] Since the year 1500, 332 species of terrestrial vertebrates have disappeared[42] and 'vertebrate species populations across the globe are, on average, about half the size they were 40 years ago'.[43] The populations of 24 of the 31 biggest carnivores on the planet (lion, leopard, puma, sea otter, dingo, lynx, bear, etc.) are in serious decline, thanks to the domino effect[44]; this dangerously disrupts the ecosystems they inhabit.[45]

At sea, the situation is particularly dramatic. There are practically no marine ecosystems left that have not been disrupted by human beings,[46] and almost half of them (41 per cent) are seriously affected.[47] In 2003, a study estimated that 90 per cent of the biomass of large fish had disappeared since the beginning of the industrial era.[48] This number, which left many scientists incredulous at the time, has now been confirmed.[49] The oceans have literally emptied. In January 2013, for example, only one specimen of bluefin tuna was sold in Tokyo – for 1.7 million dollars![50]

The same fate has befallen birds. New Zealand, for example, has lost half of its bird species[51] and, in Europe, 52 per cent of the wild bird populations have disappeared over the last three decades.[52] This rapid decline in bird populations is accentuated by the pollution caused by neonicotinoid insecticides used in agriculture (which have decimated the insects that birds feed on).[53]

Among invertebrates – not often studied in sufficient detail – two-thirds of species populations that scientists are tracking are declining (by an average of 45 per cent),[54] including wild pollinators and the honey bee.[55] 'For Mr. Bijleveld, the ongoing decline of the entire entomofauna is a "brutal collapse'".[56]

When it comes to tropical forests, due to poaching and excessive hunting, they are 'empty of wildlife', observes Richard Corlett of Xishuangbanna Tropical Botanical Garden in Menglun (China). This is a reality that we can observe in most of the lush tropical forests of the world, in Asia, Africa and Latin America. In Borneo, after thirty years of measurements in the forest of Lambir, the ecologist Rhett Harrison and his team from the World Agroforestry Centre in Kunming (China) have been able to closely observe this 'defaunation': the animals are no longer there, there is nothing left. 'There is deafening silence,' notes Carlos Peres of the University of East Anglia.[57]

To produce an extinction comparable to that which swept away the dinosaurs 65 million years ago, and for palaeontologists to talk about a 'sixth mass extinction', more than 75 per cent of the planet's species need to disappear. We are not there yet, but we are rapidly getting closer to this figure.[58] And yet society still does not recognize the decline of biodiversity as a major factor in global change on the same level as the other 'crises' that mobilize the international community, such as global heating, pollution, the hole in the ozone layer and the acidification of the oceans.[59]

But the evidence is there: domino-effect extinctions have dramatic and profound consequences for the productivity, stability and sustainability of the planet's ecosystems. As a result of our having disrupted or 'simplified' them (especially by industrial agricultural activity), these ecosystems are becoming very vulnerable and starting to collapse.[60] The idea – a simple one, after all – that diversity is essential for the stability of ecosystems (a basic lesson of scientific ecology) has apparently still not penetrated the brains of most people in the political and economic elites.

Biodiversity is the guarantor of resilient and productive agriculture and, above all, of the continuing functions of ecosystem regulation (air quality, stability of local and global climate, carbon sequestration, soil fertility and recycling of waste products), the functions connected with the supply of vital resources (fresh water, wood, medicinal substances, etc.) and cultural functions (recreational, aesthetic and spiritual). It influences human health by allowing us, for example, to control the emergence of infectious diseases,[61] as happened with the Ebola virus in 2014 that was able to spread in West Africa because of – inter alia – the destruction of forest ecosystems.[62]

And how, for example, can the function of pollination (which after all involves 75 per cent of the species cultivated in agriculture) be guaranteed in the absence of pollinating insects? By using cheap labour to pollinate fruit trees flower by flower, as is the case in the Sichuan region in China where bees have vanished?[63] By using mechanical drones, maybe? Some experts are even trying to give a monetary value to the services provided by ecosystems. In 1998, it was estimated at twice the global GDP.[64] But do these numbers mean anything? Nature obviously cannot be reduced to economics. The web of life is a matrix that cannot be replaced on a global scale by technical and industrial processes (as we have been trying to do for three centuries, with only mixed success).

It is accepted that the growth of international trade, and thus the expansion of invasive species, is one of the major causes of the decline in biodiversity.[65] But we must avoid concluding that in the case of 'de-globalization', or a collapse in the global economy, biodiversity would be in any better shape – quite the opposite.[66] During the twentieth century, despite a world population that quadrupled, human beings 'only' doubled the amount of biomass they took from ecosystems. This 'delay effect', which has preserved many forests, is due only to the massive consumption of fossil fuels.[67] In the absence of these, therefore, the populations of the whole world will rush to the forests in urgent quest of a little game, some arable land and especially firewood, as happened in Greece after the economic crisis began. The wood will probably also serve to maintain a semblance of industrial activity, given that 'it takes about 50 m³ of wood to melt 1 tonne of iron, i.e., one year of sustainable production of 10 hectares of forest'.[68] Not to mention the possibility of future wars: we know, for example, that 'in 1916–1918, when German U-boats blocked British trade relations, the United Kingdom had to cut down nearly half of its commercial forests to meet military needs.'[69]

To this, we need to add the impact of climate change, which, as most models show, will have 'dramatic' consequences on biodiversity, and could even, in the worst-case scenarios, trigger the prophesied sixth mass extinction.[70]

Biodiversity is not a luxury to which only people out for a Sunday walk – rich and cultured people, by definition – have access. The consequences of a decline in biodiversity are far more serious than we imagine. Reduce the number of species and we reduce the 'services' that ecosystems provide us with, and thereby reduce the capacity of the biosphere to sustain us. This will sooner or later result in a reduction of the human population,[71] following the usual pattern: famines, diseases and wars.

The other boundaries of the planet

Climate, biodiversity ... Unfortunately, there are many other 'boundaries'. In a highly influential study published in the journal *Nature* in 2009[72] and updated in 2015,[73] an international team of researchers tried to put a figure on nine planetary boundaries that it is absolutely vital not to cross if we are to avoid falling into a danger zone for our survival. They include, of course, climate change and the decline of biodiversity (now also known as the 'integrity of the biosphere') but also the acidification of the oceans, the depletion of stratospheric ozone, the disruption of the phosphorus and nitrogen cycles, the impact of aerosols on the atmosphere, the consumption of fresh water, changes in land use and finally chemical pollution. Seven of them have been quantified to date, and four have apparently already been exceeded. The first two, climate and biodiversity, as we have seen, can *by themselves* have a deleterious impact on human destiny. The other two are changes in land use measured by the decline of forest cover and the main bio-geochemical cycles of nitrogen and phosphorus, which have been irreversibly disrupted.[74] The quantities of these nutrients released into the soil or into the water by human activity – inter alia agricultural activity – are no longer being absorbed fast enough by natural cycles and are polluting our environment by water eutrophication. There are immediate consequences: non-drinkable water, explosions in the populations of cyanobacteria that are toxic to humans and farm animals, and the death of aquatic fauna due to lack of oxygen in the areas concerned.[75]

With regard to water, researchers have estimated, at 4,000 km^3/year, the world freshwater consumption boundary that must not be crossed if irreversible catastrophic effects are to be avoided, such as epidemics, pollution, a decline in biodiversity and the collapse of ecosystems.[76] But the most direct consequences of lack of water are food shortages, as the development of irrigation was one of the main factors of the spectacular increase in human population during the green revolution. Current global consumption is estimated at 2,600 km^3/year, but the authors indicate that the remaining room for manoeuvre is dangerously lessened because of global heating (the disappearance of the glaciers), population increase and the growth of agricultural activity (pollution and rapid depletion of non-renewable underground stocks of fresh water).[77] The remaining safety zone for the future water needs of humankind is thus very slender. Today, about 80 per cent of the world's population is at risk of shortages,[78] especially in densely populated areas such as Europe, India and China.[79]

Chemical pollution, meanwhile, is also very worrying. For some years, there has been a great deal of scientific evidence about the consequences of synthetic chemicals on human health.[80] We now know that exposure to certain synthetic chemicals during the embryonic stage modifies the expression of genes and therefore impacts on the health, morphology and physiology of future adults: a decline in fertility, rising obesity, altered behaviour, and so on.[81] But in addition to the problems caused by exposure to high doses, there is the problem of chronic exposure at very low doses, potentially affecting almost everyone on Earth. In agriculture, when manure is spread, more than 90 per cent of the product is unabsorbed by plants and ends up in the soil where some may persist for many years, contaminating waters and migrating to untreated areas.[82] Residues of insecticides (especially neonicotinoids, at present) cause collapses in insect populations, including bees,[83] but also damage to vertebrates[84] and finally to wildlife and agriculture.[85] Air pollution is another consequence, as evidenced by episodes of 'airpocalypse' in the big Chinese cities and even in Europe: for example, 'on 13 December 2013, the streets of Paris were as polluted as a 20 sq. metre room occupied by eight smokers. [...] These ultrafine particles, whose diameter is less than 0.1 micrometre (µm), are extremely harmful for human health because they penetrate deeply into the lungs, enter the bloodstream and can reach the vessels of the heart.'[86] These forms of pollution are problematic because they cause millions of deaths (and contribute to lowering our average lifespan), but they also impact on biodiversity and the functioning of the ecosystem, as well as on future generations who, in the event of economic collapse, might not be able to rely on a modern medical system.

There are many 'boundaries' and we cannot discuss all of them in detail. This is not our aim. The idea we need to take away from this overview is that we are surrounded by boundaries. Whether we are talking about climate, other species, pollution or the availability of water, crossing any of these boundaries seriously affects the health and the economy of many human populations, including the populations of industrialized countries. Worse, the disruption of any one of the systems (the climate, for example) causes upheavals in the others (biodiversity, natural cycles, the economy, etc.), which in turn impact on others in a huge domino effect that no one can control, *and that no one can see*. Boundaries show us one thing: the great industrial machine, though remarkably efficient, becomes paradoxically ever more vulnerable as it grows and gains in power.

What happens when we cross different Rubicons?

Imagine a switch on which you're exerting an increasing pressure: at first, it doesn't move, so you increase and maintain the pressure; it still doesn't move and then, at a given moment, click! It switches to a state totally different from the initial state. Just before the click, you could feel that the switch was about to yield under the pressure, but you couldn't predict the exact moment.

For ecosystems, it's (almost) the same. For a long time, it was believed that nature responded to disruptions in a gradual and proportionate manner. In reality, ecosystems also function as switches. Those which undergo regular disruptions (hunting, fishing, pollution, droughts, etc.) do not immediately show any apparent signs of wear, but gradually – and imperceptibly – lose their capacity to recover (i.e., they lose their so-called 'resilience') until reaching a tipping point, an invisible threshold beyond which the ecosystem collapses in a brutal and unpredictable way. Click! In 2001, a new discipline was born: the science of 'catastrophic shifts'.[87]

For example, a lake can quickly change from a translucent state to a completely opaque state due to the pressure of constant fishing. The gradual decrease in the number of large fish causes, at a particular moment, a domino effect throughout the food web which in the end leads to a very sudden and widespread proliferation of microalgae. This new state is very stable and difficult to reverse. The problem is that nobody had anticipated this invasion of algae, and no one *could* (until recently) predict it.

Similarly, in semi-arid forests, once enough vegetation cover has vanished, the soil dries out a little too much and triggers the violent emergence of a desert, which prevents any vegetation from growing back.[88] This is what happened to the Sahara five thousand years ago when the forest suddenly became a desert[89]; a similar transition is probably beginning in the Amazon basin.[90]

In 2008, a team of climatologists identified fourteen 'Arctic climate tipping points' where similar dramatic changes are likely (the Siberian permafrost, the currents in the Atlantic oceanic, the Amazon rainforest, the ice caps, etc.).[91] Even if some of them are reversible, or at least have been during the course of geological history,[92] each of them is able – by itself – to accelerate climate change catastrophically ... and also to trigger others. As Hans Joachim Schellnhuber, founder and director of the Potsdam Institute for Climate Impact Research (PIK), points out, 'the responses of the Earth system to climate change seem to be non-linear. If we venture beyond the threshold of +2°C, towards the bar of +4°C, the risk of exceeding the tipping points increases sharply'.

This approach applies very well to agricultural systems and human systems, which also include ecological, economic and sociocultural breaking points: the management of dry forests in Madagascar (whose destruction is wrecking the local economy), the production of Fédou cheese in the Causses region (whose pastoral system is very fragile) and the emergence of 'buzz' on social networks.[93]

The presence of these tipping points is often due to the great connectivity and homogeneity of systems (see chapter 7) associated with domino effects and feedback loops. Indeed, a complex living system (ecosystems, organizations, societies, economies, markets, etc.) consists of countless interwoven feedback loops that keep the system stable and relatively resilient. When approaching a break point, just one small disruption, such as a drop of water, is enough for certain loops to change nature and drag the entire system into an unpredictable and often irreversible chaos. Either the system dies or it reaches another state of equilibrium, admittedly more resilient and more stable, but often very uncomfortable (for us).

At a global level, the global economic system and the Earth system are two complex systems subject to the same non-linear dynamics and also containing tipping points. This is brought out in two recent studies, one analysing the risks of a global systemic financial crisis system that would cause a major economic collapse in a very short period of time,[94] and the other considering the possibility that the 'global ecosystem' is coming dangerously close to a threshold beyond which life on Earth would become impossible for the majority of the species present.[95] This is the well-known study published in 2012 in the journal *Nature* by an international team of 24 researchers: it caused a great stir with the media (exaggeratedly) predicting 'the end of the world in 2100'.[96] Even if such global tipping points have already been reached in the past[97] (five mass extinctions, transitions to ice ages, and changes in the composition of the atmosphere preceding the explosion of life in the Cambrian), the authors indicate that they have been rare, and that nothing about the present situation can be certain given the complexity of the case as well as the difficulties in measuring all the parameters.[98] However, they bring together a cluster of indices showing that we humans have the ability to devastate the entire Earth system radically and rapidly and that we are well on the way to doing so.

This nascent science of catastrophic change is remarkable because it totally changes our understanding of the gravity of the upheavals that our model of industrial development triggers. We now know that every year that passes, and thus every small step towards an intensification of 'crises', does not produce foreseeable proportional effects, but increases the risks of sudden, unpredictable and irreversible catastrophes *more than proportionally*.

4

Is the Steering Locked?

Do you know the origin of the QWERTY (and AZERTY) arrangement of letters on the keyboards that we all use? For the answer, you have to go back to the time of the old typewriters that used a scrolling ink ribbon struck by metal blocks placed at the end of slender stems. The layout of the letters has a very precise function, thought out by the engineers of the time: it keeps the rhythm of the stems as constant as possible so that they do not get tangled. So some of the most common letters in the English language were given to weaker fingers to type in order to homogenize the strike rhythm.[1]

Today, flat digital keyboards no longer need such precautions. Some engineers have invented a new type of keyboard, much faster and more powerful than QWERTY: DVORAK. But who uses a DVORAK keyboard? Nobody. So we find ourselves in an absurd situation where the old typewriters have disappeared but where everyone still uses the old technical system that came with them, though it is less efficient for our own times.

In a completely different field, it has now been clearly demonstrated that alternative farming systems, such as agro-ecology, permaculture and bio-intensive micro-agriculture,[2] can produce – with much less energy – yields per hectare comparable with or even superior to industrial agriculture over smaller surfaces, while restoring soils and ecosystems by reducing the impact on the climate and by restructuring peasant communities.[3] The Grupo de Agricultura Orgánica (GAO) of Cuba received the alternative Nobel Prize (Right Livelihood Award) in 1999 for demonstrating this in a concrete, large-scale way.[4] Today, agroecology is even recognized and promoted by the UN[5] and the Food and Agriculture Organization (FAO).[6] So why haven't these powerful and credible alternatives taken off? Why are we still 'prisoners' of industrial agriculture?

The answer lies in the very structure of our system of innovation. In fact, when a new and more efficient technology makes its appearance, it does not automatically become the norm – far from it. Indeed, it is often very difficult to change systems because of a phenomenon that historians and sociologists of innovation call sociotechnical 'lock-in'.

We all stop at the petrol station to fill our tanks because our ancestors (some of them) decided *at a certain point* to generalize the use of the thermal engine, the car and oil. We are stuck in the technological choices of these ancestors. Current technological trajectories are therefore largely determined by our past and, quite often, technological innovations are just trying to solve the problems caused by previous ones. This 'path-dependent' evolution can, in many ways, lead to 'technological dead-ends', trapping us in increasingly counterproductive choices.

How a system becomes locked in

Let's take two other examples, the electric system and car transport.[7] In the first case, when one or several thermal electric power plants are installed in a region, this triggers a self-reinforcing cycle. The government, through economic incentives or favourable legislation, perpetuates the system of electricity production by allowing investors to develop it and therefore predict the generation of later and more efficient power plants. Gradually, the growth of this technical system generates economies of scale and lower costs which, in turn, increase the availability of the system for a greater number of users. In so doing, the electric system becomes part of consumers' habits, and the price of electricity, which has become affordable, promotes not only its expansion but also fosters a growing consumption of energy. Then this sociotechnical system becomes widespread and gives rise to a multitude of secondary innovations that improve it and consolidate it. Finally, as demand grows, the government take measures favourable to its expansion and so on, thus increasing the dominance of the electric system. Lock-in appears when new technical niches, for example alternative and more efficient energy systems, can no longer emerge *because* the dominant energy system leaves no space for diversity.

For car transport, a similar cycle has been established. By promoting ever-denser road infrastructures, governments are increasing the use already made of them by drivers (because they can always go farther and faster), and allow new users to benefit from these infrastructures. The increasing use of the road system promotes investment and public support. Tax revenue grows steadily, allowing the system to expand and even to destroy other more efficient transport systems, as in the United States with the destruction of the tram system in the early twentieth century by General Motors, Standard Oil and Firestone, with the help of the government.[8]

The self-referential side of this process is fundamental. The more this dominant system becomes entrenched, the more it has the means to maintain its dominance. It swallows up all the available resources and 'mechanically' prevents the emergence of alternatives, whereas it is precisely in its early stages that an innovation needs support and investment. In other words, the 'small shoots' are not able to compete with the big tree that provides them with shade. The tragedy is that, by preventing small systems on the margins from blossoming, we deprive ourselves of potential solutions for the future.

Lock-in mechanisms are numerous and very various. First, there are the purely technical aspects. For example, a dominant system can decide on the compatibility (or not) of objects introduced to the market by small emerging competitors, as is often the case in the field of computing.

There are also psychological aspects. For example, a research team from the University of Indiana has shown that investments in innovative technology design depended more on the trajectories of the past than on desires for the future.[9] Investors are not as reckless as we might think: they tend to prefer investing in what already works and what engineers can improve, rather than in an unknown system that has not yet won its spurs. This could explain, incidentally, why we find it so difficult to try out new and truly innovative political systems ... In the same spirit, one very important psychological obstacle is related to the inertia of individual behaviour and the reluctance of individuals to change. When a system is implanted, it creates habits that we have trouble getting rid of: plastic bags in supermarkets, the 70 mph maximum speed limit on motorways, and so on.

There are also institutional mechanisms, such as legal and regulatory frameworks, that prevent the emergence of new 'sociotechnical niches': these include the regulation of agricultural pesticides, blocking the development of natural products, and the seed laws that stifle innovative seed techniques in peasant communities. Then there is the difficulty governments have in abandoning major grant programmes. At the global level, for example, the total grants awarded to fossil fuels came to US$550 billion in 2013 (against US$120 billion for renewable energies).[10] The institutional inertia of a system is also reflected in the construction of large ecologically destructive and economically useless projects, where huge investments are committed on the basis of decisions dating back to a time when conditions (economic, social and environmental) were not the same as today. Finally, another institutional lock-in mechanism is simply the existence of very heavy infrastructures related to a source of energy. Indeed, the recycling of nuclear power plants and oil refineries is no easy matter! Changing energy type is like giving up everything that institutions have invested in and built up in the past, and which still has economic and social consequences for the present and the future. In social psychology, this 'hidden trap' mechanism[11] refers to the tendency of individuals to persevere in an action, even when this becomes unreasonably expensive or no longer achieves its objectives. In terms of emotional life, for example, it's the tendency to stay with a partner we no longer love, as 'we can't have gone through all those years for nothing'.

But, some will retort, isn't the *raison d'être* of an institution precisely to *preserve* an accumulated heritage, a sociotechnical trajectory, a certain social order? Certainly: but the problem is that it is precisely the institutions dedicated to innovation (public and private research) which are monopolized by the dominant sociotechnical system.

In the agronomic sciences, for example, a PhD student in agroecology will find his or her path strewn with far more obstacles and yielding far fewer credits than a PhD student in agrochemistry or genetic engineering[12] – let alone the fact that it will be much harder to publish in 'prestigious' scientific journals, making it more difficult to make a career in research. This leads Jean Gadrey, former professor of economics at the University of Lille, to protest: 'Try entrusting [the agriculture of the future] to an academy of "best experts" at the INRA [the French National Institute for Agricultural Research] where, out of nine thousand positions, there are only thirty-five jobs in full-time equivalent posts in research on organic farming!'[13]

Lock-in mechanisms can also be identified in the principles of collective action. For example, citizens involved in the fight against global heating and in building a 'post-carbon' world can be counted in the tens of millions (we can see this in consciousness-raising campaigns, demonstrations, petitions and debates), but they are scattered and uncoordinated (not to mention the fact that, like everyone, they use fossil fuels to live). Conversely, far fewer people are engaged in producing energy from fossil fuels. The Total group, for example, has a hundred thousand employees (some of whom are probably convinced that we must fight against global heating) who are much better organized and can draw on considerable funds (a gross figure of 22.4 billion euros' worth of investment in 2013). In short, an established technical system provides itself with the means to resist change.

Let's not be naive. The lock-in is not just 'mechanical', it is also the result of intense lobbying campaigns. In France, for example, in order to be able to 'evacuate' nuclear generation of electricity (which is very difficult to store), some entrepreneurs still suggest installing electric heating in the new constructions, even though this makes no thermodynamic sense. (Since electricity is a 'noble' energy, it can be used for many things other than just heat.) These campaigns can even transgress the legal framework. In 1968, General Electric practised aggressive marketing to impose this same type of heating on real-estate developers, 'even threatening the promoters that they would not connect their housing lots if they supplied any other sources of energy'.[14] The development of solar energy in the United States in those years was therefore stifled even though it constituted a better technical solution. In the same way, to push the peasant world into the system of pesticides (the so-called 'green revolution'), agrochemical firms had to deploy considerable energy and spend insane amounts of money,[15] as evidenced by the images of entomologists who went so far as to drink DDT in front of the sceptics to prove it wasn't toxic![16]

However, as these last examples prove, some lock-ins sooner or later break down. In fact, they often merely delay transitions.[17] The problem today is that we can no longer allow ourselves to wait, and the lock-ins have become immense.

The problem of complexity

Where the problem becomes serious is that the globalization, interconnection and homogenization of the economy have tightened the lock-in by radically intensifying the power of the systems already in place. According to archaeologist Joseph Tainter, this apparently inexorable tendency of societies to move towards greater levels of complexity, specialization and sociopolitical control is even one of the major causes of the collapse of societies.[18] Indeed, over time, societies gradually turn towards natural resources that become increasingly expensive as they are more difficult to exploit (the easiest being exhausted first), thereby reducing their energy benefits at the very same time as they are increasing their bureaucracy, social control spending at home and military budgets simply in order to maintain the status quo. Locked in by all this complexity, the metabolism of a society reaches a threshold of diminishing returns that makes it more and more vulnerable to collapse.

By becoming globalized, our industrial society has reached extreme levels of complexity; indeed, as we saw earlier, it is entering a phase of diminishing returns. But above all, it has dangerously extended its sociotechnical lock-ins. Indeed, once a system is established in a region or a country, it becomes economically very competitive or even technically efficient and spreads rapidly to other countries through knock-on effects. The effectiveness of the systems in place then makes it difficult to break out of this paradigm, especially when competition between all countries becomes the rule. This 'global lock-in'[19] can be illustrated by three examples: the financial system; the energy system based on carbon; and growth.

In recent years, finance has been concentrated in a small number of huge financial institutions.[20] In Great Britain, for example, the market share of the three largest banks rose from 50 per cent in 1997 to almost 80 per cent in 2008. This phenomenon of concentration has obliged states to give implicit bank guarantees, which has eroded market discipline and encouraged banks to take excessive risks; besides this, the links between these institutions and governments are now 'very close'. That's how some financial institutions and multinationals[21] have become 'too big to fail' or 'too big to jail'.

The history of carbon and its techno-industrial complex is probably the biggest lock-in in history. 'The "initial conditions", the abundance of coal and oil, but also political decisions encouraging one source of energy rather than another [have determined] technological trajectories over a very long period.'[22] Today, if we take away oil, gas and coal, there is not much left of our thermo-industrial civilization. Almost everything we are familiar with depends on it: transport, food, clothing, heating, and so on. The economic and political power of oil and gas majors has become disproportionate, to such an extent that 90 global companies have alone been responsible for 63 per cent of greenhouse gas emissions worldwide since 1751.[23] Worse, proponents of the energy transition (towards renewables) need this thermal power to build an alternative energy system. This produces a somewhat droll paradox: if it can hope to survive, our civilization must fight against the sources of its own power and stability, thereby shooting itself in the foot! When the survival of civilization totally depends on a dominant technical system, it's the ultimate lock-in.

Locking in growth follows the same logic. The stability of the debt system rests entirely on this growth: the world economic system cannot abandon it if it wants to carry on working. This means that we need growth to continue to repay credits, to pay pensions and even to prevent the rise of unemployment.[24] In fact, none of our institutions is adapted to a world without growth because they were designed *for* and *by* growth. It's like trying to slow down a rocket on the way up, bringing it back down and landing it gently.... If we are deprived of growth for too long, the economic system implodes under mountains of debt that will never be repaid. But, as with carbon, for the global economic system to be transformed with flexibility and agility, it needs to work optimally, i.e., with strong growth. Then you can savour this other paradox: it is therefore difficult to envisage a *controlled* contraction of the global economic system. And the corollary: what the transition needs to be able to deploy quickly is strong economic growth.

The intensity and ubiquity of these sociotechnical lock-ins have made the people who depend on them – us! – extremely heterogeneous, that is to say, we lack the ability to pull the plug or simply to try and find a few islands of autonomy. The political world too, structurally oriented towards short-term choices, has little room for manoeuvre. As Barack Obama admits, 'I think the American people right now have been so focused, and will continue to be focused on our economy and jobs and growth, that if the message is somehow we're going to ignore jobs and growth simply to address climate change, I don't think anybody is going to go for that. I won't go for that.'[25]

We (especially our ancestors) have created gigantic and monstrous systems that have become indispensable for maintaining the living conditions of billions of people. Not only do these systems prevent any transition, they cannot even afford to let themselves be tampered with in case they collapse. Since the system is self-referential, it is obvious that we will not be able to find solutions *within* the dominant system. We must cultivate innovations on the margins. That's the whole purpose of a transition. But are there any margins left?

To sum up, we have very quickly climbed the ladder of technical progress and complexity in what could be considered a self-perpetuating headlong flight. Today, while the height of the ladder of progress may make us feel giddy, many people are realizing – with horror – that its bottom rungs have disappeared and that the ascent is continuing inexorably nonetheless. It's no longer possible to stop this upwards movement and come down quietly to find a less complex lifestyle on terra firma – unless we jump off the ladder, which will involve a shock for the person jumping or indeed trigger a major systemic shock if lots of people fall off the ladder at the same time.[26] Those who understand this are filled with anxiety that the further their ascent continues, the more painful will be their fall.

5

Trapped in an Ever More Fragile Vehicle

Several hundred thousand bolts, nuts and rivets of different sizes, tens of thousands of metal parts for engines and bodywork, rubber, plastic and carbon fibre parts, thermosetting polymers, fabrics, glass, microprocessors.... In total, six million parts are needed to build a Boeing 747. To assemble its aircraft, Boeing uses nearly 6,500 suppliers, based in more than a hundred countries, and performs approximately 360,000 business transactions every month.[1] Such is the amazing complexity of our modern world.

In the space of fifty years, we have seen most parts of the world becoming globally interconnected. Information, finance, trade and its supply chains, tourism and the infrastructures on which these flows rely – all these systems have become closely connected.

For physicist Yaneer Bar-Yam, research scientist at the MIT Media Laboratory and director of the New England Complex Systems Institute in Cambridge, Massachusetts, 'A networked society behaves like a multicellular organism'.[2]

Most of the organs are vital; you can't amputate a single part without risking the death of the whole organism. What Bar-Yam discovered was that the more complex these systems are, the more vital each organ becomes for the whole organism. At the global level, therefore, all the sectors and all the regions of our globalized civilization have become interdependent to the point where one of them cannot suffer from a collapse without making the whole metaorganism vulnerable. In other words, our living conditions *at this precise time and in this precise place* depend on what happened *a short time ago* in many places on Earth. This suggests that, as Bar-Yam points out, '[industrial] civilization is very vulnerable'.[3]

There are three main categories of risk that threaten the stability of a complex system: threshold effects ('all or nothing' phenomena), domino effects (or contagion effects), and the inability of the system to recover its balance after a shock (the phenomenon of hysteresis).[4] As we have seen, these risks are present in the natural systems on which we depend but they also exist in our own systems, as we will see for finance, supply chains and the physical infrastructures that shape our societies.

Finance: feet of clay

As we have already seen, the international financial system has become a complex network of debts and obligations that connects the balance sheets of a large number of intermediaries.[5] We can measure this complexification by the growing body of regulations that have had to be set up to manage it. For example, the Basel Accords, which aim to guarantee a minimum level of equity in order to ensure the financial soundness of the banks, contained 30 pages in 1988 (Basel I), 347 in 2004 (Basel II), and 616 in 2010 (Basel III). The documents necessary to implement these agreements between signatory countries, for example, the United States, ran to 18 pages in 1998 and now contain about 30,000 pages![6]

The system has also gained in speed and sophistication. Thanks to high frequency trading, buying and selling orders can be effected automatically at speeds of the order of a millionth of a second using ever more powerful computers.[7] Operators have also innovated by developing new financial products, derivatives (the credit default swap, or CDS, and collateralized debt obligation, or CDO), the volume of which has soared. According to the statistics of the Bank for International Settlements (BIS), the derivatives market rose to 710,000 billion in December 2013,[8] approximately ten times the size of world GDP.

The problem is that the concentration of actors, the complexity and speed of the financial system and the growing gap between regulation and traders' 'innovations' have made the financial system very fragile.[9] Shocks can now spread very rapidly to the whole network.[10] But also, complexity can itself trigger a crisis: when the economic conditions deteriorate (due to the bankruptcy of customers or a reduction in the market value of the assets they hold), banks find it so difficult to evaluate all their connections with other banks that a general mistrust sets in and provokes a fire sale, which ends with a freeze on transactions.[11] This is what happened in 2008.

Worse still, to avoid an economic collapse after this last crisis, governments have taken so-called 'unconventional' measures. Panic-stricken by the extent of the crisis, the central banks proceeded to quantitative easing, the modern equivalent of printing banknotes. They bought treasury bills (which amounts to lending to the state) and other financial securities, which allowed them to facilitate the flow of money on the markets and thus avoid total paralysis of the sector. Thus the cumulative balance sheet of the major central banks worldwide (US, European, Chinese, British and Japanese) went from 7,000 billion before the crisis to more than 14 trillion today.[12] All this money denotes no actual value. And the trend shows no real sign of losing momentum: the Japanese central bank, for example, recently decided to accelerate its policy of purchasing treasury bills to the sum of US$734 billion per year.[13] Intended to fight the deflationary spiral in progress, this strategy looks more and more like a 'currency war', in which countries respond in turn to their 'adversaries' by devaluing their currencies to promote their industries, their exports and hence their employment rates. But, according to Keynes, 'there is no more sure way to subvert the existing base of society than to debauch the currency. The process engages all the occult forces of economic law in a drive towards destruction, and does so in a way that not one man in a million can diagnose.'[14]

The trouble is that banking and monetary crises are not limited to the financial sector alone. They affect economic activity by destroying social cohesion and consumer confidence. Economies fall into recession, which in turn increases the states' deficits. The Eurozone, for example, has seen its public debt rise by more than 3 trillion euros (+50 per cent) in the space of six years, settling at a total of 9,000 billion euros, or 90 per cent of its GDP.[15] If some people now claim that economic activity managed to stabilize after this considerable effort, countries have not seen any decline in their unemployment figures, nor a lessening of social tensions. Quite the opposite …

Supply chains on the razor's edge

Over the last decades, the real economy has also become tightly interconnected through the establishment of a huge network of supply chains that facilitates the continuous flow of goods and services, from producers to consumers. Today, companies operate 'internationally': to maximize profits, they relocate and subcontract everything they can. Their new management practices focus on efficiency (the hunt for 'hidden costs') and favour just-in-time supplies to avoid keeping stocks when they become too expensive. The last vital stocks of oil and food still owned by states are only enough to hold out for a few days or even a few weeks. In the case of oil, for example, France has the obligation to stock at least 90 days' worth of net imports.[16]

By increasing the length and connectivity of these supply chains, and reducing stocks to nil, the global economic system has gained in efficiency what it has lost in resilience. As for finance, the least disruption can now cause considerable damage and spread like wildfire through the whole economy. The example of the 2011 floods in Thailand speaks volumes. Following heavy rains and four intense tropical storms, many Thai companies, from agriculture to computer and microchip manufacture, were affected by the floods. In this great rice-producing country, the annual output collapsed by 20 per cent; the worldwide production of hard drives dropped by 28 per cent, which made prices soar; the production of computers and digital photo and video recorders stopped. Rising water also devastated the Honda, Nissan and Toyota factories, which all had to stop production. In 2012, the World Economic Forum pointed out that this was all due to the fact that 'the expansion in global supply chains has greatly increased the possibility of production disruption from such disasters'.[17]

Potential sources of disruption to supply chains can be of natural origin (earthquakes, tsunamis, hurricanes, etc.) but also of human origin, due to administrative errors or terrorist acts. In January 2012, the national strategy of the White House for supply chain security was preoccupied by the need to protect the system from 'intentional attacks, accidents, or natural disasters' and the 'exploitation of the system by those seeking to introduce harmful products or materials and disruptions' such as 'criminal networks and terrorists.'[18] Already in 2004, US Secretary of Health Tommy Thompson had declared, 'I, for the life of me, cannot understand why the terrorists have not, you know, attacked our food supply because it is so easy to do.'[19] The following year, a team from Stanford University showed that using botulinum toxin to contaminate a single silo of 200,000 litres of milk in the United States could kill 250,000 people, even before the origin of the contamination had been discovered.[20]

Some researchers have described how globalized supply chains contributed to the collapse of world trade in the 2008 crisis.[21] Others have developed macroeconomic models to try and understand these knock-on mechanisms.[22] They are discovering that, like the global financial situation, knock-on effects in the supply networks can now be compared to the domino effects of trophic chains (which we discussed in chapter 2 on biodiversity).[23] A shock such as the insolvency of a supplier spreads vertically and then horizontally as it destabilizes competitors. To crown it all, supply chains are all the more fragile as they depend on the good health of the financial system that provides the credit lines necessary to any economic activity.

Infrastructures at their last gasp

Let's take the argument further. Supply networks and financial systems operate on a physical basis, namely infrastructure networks, which are also becoming increasingly more sophisticated and interconnected. These are networks of road, sea, air and rail transport but also electricity and telecommunications networks (including the internet).

These physical infrastructures are the main pillars of our societies, and are (surprise, surprise!) also prone to increased risks of systemic vulnerability. For example, all global banking transactions go through a small organization called SWIFT (the BIC code), which has only three data centres, one in the United States, one in the Netherlands and a new one in Switzerland. It provides standardized interbank transfer messaging services and interfaces to more than 10,500 institutions in more than 225 countries, for a total figure of daily transactions amounting to thousands of billions of dollars.[24] If, for one reason or another, such as terrorist attacks or cyberattacks, these nerve centres are affected, the consequences could be dramatic for the whole economy.

Transport networks are also potential vectors of instability. For example, the eruption of the Icelandic volcano Eyjafjallajökull in 2010 forced air carriers to suspend traffic for six consecutive days, significantly affecting global trade. Among all the consequences of this eruption, one was job losses in Kenya, while another was the cancellation of several surgical procedures in Ireland, and a third the stoppage of three lines of BMW production in Germany.[25]

In 2000, following the increase in diesel prices, 150 striking truckers blocked the main fuel depots in Great Britain. Just four days after the start of the strike, most of the country's refineries had stopped their activities, forcing the government to take steps to protect the remaining reserves. The next day, people rushed into supermarkets and grocery stores to stock up on food. A day later, 90 per cent of service stations were out of fuel and the National Health Service began to cancel non-essential surgical operations. Royal Mail postal deliveries stopped and schools in many towns and villages closed their doors. The big supermarkets like Tesco and Sainsbury's introduced a rationing system, and the government called in the army to escort convoys of vital goods. Finally, the strikers stopped their action as a result of public pressure.[26] According to Alan McKinnon, the author of an analysis of this event and Emeritus Professor of Logistics at Heriot-Watt University in Edinburgh, if the same thing were to happen again, 'After a week, the country would be plunged into a deep economic and social crisis. Once the lorries started running again, it would take several weeks for most production and distribution systems to recover' – and some businesses never would.[27] A report by the American Trucking Association,[28] which shares these concerns, illustrates the same point with a chronological description of the domino effects that could occur (see Box 5.1).

Refineries supply the fuel needed for road transport but also for trains supplying the main power plants with coal. Now the latter, which provide 30 per cent of Britain's electricity, 50 per cent of that in the United States and 85 per cent of that in Australia, on average have twenty days of coal reserves.[29] But without electricity, it is impossible to operate coal mines or oil pipelines. And it's also impossible to maintain running-water distribution systems, refrigeration chains, communication systems, and computer and banking centres.

A recent study by university researchers at the University of Auckland has counted about 50 major power blackouts that affected 26 countries over the last decade.[30] The researchers note that such power failures are caused by the

Box 5.1 When Trucks Stop, the United States Stops

Chronology of the deterioration in the main sectors of activity when trucks stop running:

During the first 24 hours:
- The delivery of medical supplies will stop in the affected area.
- Hospitals will run out of basic supplies such as syringes and catheters.
- Service stations will start to run out of fuel.
- Factories that work on a just-in-time basis will suffer a shortage of parts.
- The post and other parcel deliveries will cease.

After one day:
- Food shortages will appear.
- Fuels will no longer be readily available, leading to soaring prices and long queues at service stations.
- Without the parts necessary for factories and trucks for the delivery of products, the assembly lines will stop, laying off thousands of workers.

After two to three days:
- Food shortages will worsen, in particular if consumers panic and start hoarding food.
- Essential supplies like bottled water, powdered milk and canned meat will disappear from large retailers.
- Cash machines will run out of banknotes and banks will not be able to handle certain transactions.
- Service stations will run out of fuel.
- Rubbish bins will overflow in urban and suburban areas.
- Container ships will be stuck in ports and rail transport will be disrupted before coming to a halt.

After a week:
- Travel by car will be impossible due to lack of fuel. Without cars or buses, many people will be unable to get to work, to access medical care or to reach the shops.
- Hospitals will start to exhaust their reserves of oxygen.

After two weeks:
- Drinking water will start to run out.

After four weeks:
- The country will have exhausted its drinking water and all water will need to be boiled before drinking. Consequently, gastrointestinal diseases will increase, increasing the pressure on an already weakened health-care system.

fragility of networks that cannot cope with intermittent supplies of renewable energy, the depletion of fossil fuels or extreme weather events. The consequences of these failures are the same everywhere: electricity rationing, financial and economic damage, risks to food safety, dysfunctional transport, breakdowns in treatment plants and GSM antennae, and an increase in crimes and social unrest.

In addition, many transport, electricity and water-supply networks in OECD countries are now more than 50 years old (in some cases more than a century) and are already working beyond their maximum capacities.[31] Since the economic crisis of 2008, it is not uncommon to see governments delaying or freezing the investments necessary for their maintenance and the construction of new networks, which makes the infrastructure system all the more vulnerable. In the United States, for example, 70 thousand bridges (one in nine) are considered structurally deficient and 32 per cent of the roads are in poor condition.[32] This has led Ray LaHood, former secretary of transportation in Obama's presidency, to say, 'Our infrastructure is currently on a drip. [...] It's falling into ruin because we haven't made the necessary investments and we don't have the money [to do so]'.[33]

The lesson to be learned from all these examples is simple: the higher the level of interdependence of infrastructures, the more consequences small disruptions can have across a city or a country.

What will be the spark?

So far, we have seen that these systemic risks took the shape of limited losses and temporary blockages at very localized spots and specific times. The question now is whether a disruption in the financial system, supply chains or infrastructures can spread to the entire global economy and bring about its collapse.

According to David Korowicz, a systemic risk specialist, the answer is yes, and the spark could come from two places.[34] The first is the oil peak, which would jeopardize our monetary system of fractional reserves (based on debt), as we saw in chapter 2. The second is an overall imbalance in the financial system. In both cases, the global economic collapse would first involve a phase of generalized loss of confidence, itself caused by the insolvency of states and banks.

To support this, Korowicz describes a scenario of knock-on effects, starting with the disordered bankruptcy of a state in the euro area. This 'crisis' would sow panic in the banking sector country by country and then affect whole economies, in other words all sectors of activity, eventually mutating into food shortages after a few days. In less than two weeks, the crisis would spread exponentially across the world. After three weeks, some vital sectors would no longer be able to reboot their activities (see chapter 9).

In another vein, a severe pandemic could also be the cause of a major collapse.[35] For this, there is no need for a virus that would wipe out 99 per cent of humankind: just a small percentage would suffice. Indeed, when a society becomes more complex, the specialization of tasks intensifies, producing key functions without which society cannot manage. Examples include road hauliers who supply the country with fuel; certain technical jobs in nuclear power plants; and engineers who maintain computer hubs. For Bar-Yam, 'One of the most profound results of complex systems research is that when systems are highly complex, individuals matter.'[36]

According to Jon Lay, who heads a global emergency team at Exxon Mobil which simulated the effects of a return of the 1918 flu pandemic, 'We think that if we can make people feel safe about coming to work, we'll have about 25 per cent staff absences if we get a flu pandemic like the one in 1918.'[37] In this case, if everything is done to preserve important jobs, there will be no serious consequences. 'If we have 50 per cent absences, it's a different story.' And if we include not just the sick but those who stay at home because they are afraid of the pandemic, the domino effects could be catastrophic. After a few days, the whole system might implode. In 2006, economists simulated the effects of the 1918 flu pandemic on today's world. The result: 142 million deaths worldwide, and an economic recession that would lop 12.6 per cent off global GDP.[38] In this scenario, the mortality rate was 3 per cent (of infected people). However, for the H5N1 virus or for Ebola, the rate can exceed 50–60 per cent.

Some will argue that, in the Middle Ages, the plague wiped out one-third of the European population, but this did not lead to the extinction of civilization. That is true, but the situation was different. Societies were much less complex than they are today. Not only were regional economies compartmentalized, thereby reducing the risk of knock-on effects, but the population consisted of a majority of peasants. Now, a decrease of one-third of peasants reduces agricultural production by a third, but does eliminate functions that are vital to society as a whole – not to mention that, at that time, survivors could still rely on unpolluted and diversified ecosystems, new potential arable land, relatively abundant forests and a stable climate. Today, these conditions are no longer met.

Moreover, it seems that to date few people have become aware of the systemic aspect of things, and governments are turning out to be particularly inefficient at finding solutions.[39] For their part, 'international institutions are concentrating mainly on simple problems, ignoring the interactions of the entire system. Fighting against climate change through forest plantations, for example, can destroy the ecosystems targeted by the Convention on Biodiversity of the United Nations. [Or else] the promotion of biofuels can accelerate deforestation and erode the food security of poor countries'.[40]

Finally, it is important to point out that systems have become so complex that even in the absence of external shocks, and just as a result of their structure, they can suffer collapse. Indeed, beyond a certain level of complexity, the technological measuring tools are not even powerful enough to understand and predict the chaotic behaviour of such super-systems. It has simply become impossible to control them completely[41]: even if experts and decision makers are informed about the risks (which is not always the case), are competent (ditto) and have the best technologies, they cannot avoid systemic disruptions to global networks.

This 'hyperglobalization', then, has transformed the global economy into a highly complex gigantic system that connects and multiplies the risks specific to each of the critical sectors we have discussed. This has brought a new type of risk, *global systemic risk*, which can be triggered by countless potential factors – a risk that can rapidly entail both small recessions and a major economic crisis or widespread collapse.

In our societies, very few people these days can manage without a supermarket, credit card or petrol station. When a civilization becomes 'uprooted' – in other words, when a majority of its inhabitants no longer have a direct link with the Earth system (earth, water, wood, animals, plants, etc.) – the population becomes entirely dependent on the artificial structure that maintains it in this state. If this ever more powerful but vulnerable structure collapses, it's the survival of the entire population that may be endangered.

Summary of Part I

An all-too-clear picture

Let's pause for breath. And summarize what we've said so far.

To maintain itself and avoid financial disorder and social unrest, our industrial civilization is forced to accelerate, to become more complex and to consume ever more energy. Its dazzling expansion has been nurtured by the exceptional availability (though this will not last long) of fossil fuels that are very energy efficient, coupled with a growth economy and highly unstable levels of debt. But the growth of our industrial civilization, today constrained by geophysical and economic limits, has reached a phase of decreasing returns. Technology, which has long served to push these limits back, is less and less able to ensure this acceleration and 'locks in' this unsustainable trajectory by preventing the development of new alternatives.

At the same time, the sciences of complexity are discovering that, beyond certain thresholds, complex systems – including economies and ecosystems – suddenly switch to new and unpredictable states of equilibrium and may even collapse. We are more and more aware that we have crossed certain 'boundaries' that guaranteed the stability of our living conditions, as a society and as a species. The global climate system, and many of the planet's ecosystems and major biogeochemical cycles, have left the zone of stability that we were familiar with heralding a time of sudden large-scale disruptions which in turn will destabilize industrial societies, the rest of humankind and even all other species.

The paradox that characterizes our era – and probably all eras when civilizations came up against limits and crossed boundaries – is that the more powerful our civilization grows, the more vulnerable it becomes. The modern globalized political, social and economic system, which provides half of humankind with life, has seriously depleted the resources and disrupted the systems on which it relied – the climate and ecosystems – to such an extent that it has dangerously undermined the conditions that formerly allowed it to expand and guarantee its stability and survival.

At the same time, the ever more globalized, interconnected and locked-in structure of our civilization not only makes it highly vulnerable to the slightest internal or external disruption but now subjects it to processes of systemic collapse.

That's the situation we are in. To preserve ourselves from serious disruptions to the climate and the ecosystems (the disruptions that threaten the species), we need to turn off the engine. The only route to follow if we are to find a safe space for ourselves, then, is to stop in its tracks the production and consumption of fossil fuels, as these lead to economic and probably political and social collapse, and ultimately to the end of thermo-industrial civilization.

To save the engine of our industrial civilization, we have to cross more and more boundaries, i.e., continue to prospect, dig, produce and grow ever faster. This inevitably leads to climatic, ecological and biogeophysical tipping points, and to a peak in resources, and so ultimately to the same result – economic collapse – albeit one that might also involve a collapse of the human species, even almost all living species.

Today, we are sure of four things: (1) the physical growth of our societies will come to a halt in the near future; (2) we have irreversibly damaged the entire Earth system (at least on the geological scale of human beings); (3) we are moving towards a very unstable, 'non-linear' future, where major disruptions (internal and external) will be the norm; and (4) we are now potentially subject to global systemic collapses.

So, like many economists, climatologists, physicists, agronomists, ecologists, soldiers, journalists, philosophers and even politicians (including some we quoted in the epigraphs to this book), we deduce that our society may collapse in the near future.

To resume the metaphor of the car, while the rate of acceleration has never been so high, the fuel levels indicate that we're falling back on our reserves and the engine is drawing its last breath and has started smoking and coughing. Intoxicated by speed, we leave the marked trail and, in conditions of near-zero visibility, plunge down a steep slope riddled with obstacles. Some passengers realize that the car is very fragile but apparently not the driver, who continues to press the pedal to the metal!

Seeing this picture as a whole, and not through one or more 'crises' taken separately, represents a qualitative leap in the way we understand our era. The example of the Ebola virus is interesting (in the following, the crises are in brackets): forest destruction (biodiversity) favoured the spread of the virus (health) but the number of people killed or rendered unfit for work and the measures to contain the disease have slowed down economic activity (economy) and seriously disrupted the supply networks (infrastructure) and harvests (food). The result is that less than six months after the epidemic broke out, more than a million people are threatened by hunger in West Africa[1] and the Guinean health service is severely weakened [infrastructure].[2] What will happen in the next epidemic if industrial health services are no longer capable of providing a solution?

Similarly, faced with an alarming figure, for example the oil peak, the reflex of our reductionist scientific culture is to spontaneously look for 'solutions' in the same domain, even if these are often incompatible with connected 'crises'. If we are aware of the interconnections between all the relevant areas, we will avoid such pitfalls and also see that there are rarely any technical 'solutions' that do not worsen the situation by consuming more energy and materials.

The picture has become so obvious, so huge and overwhelming, that even if by chance some researchers are mistaken in their conclusions, if one or other of them is wrong or if we have ventured into an erroneous interpretation, the argument remains substantially the same and the conclusion is undeniable. Imagine an ideal world where we succeed in controlling finance. Would that change anything about the frequency of hurricanes, the end of oil, the length of supply chains or the extinction of animal species? Let's imagine that we were to find, tomorrow, a new source of boundless energy, how could we avoid the end of phosphate ores,[3] population displacement or global systemic risks due to globalization? True, we could maybe maintain a semblance of industrial civilization for a few more years, but we would probably then simply fall from a greater height ...

During our research, we progressively had the feeling of being hemmed in on all sides. Worse, we found that all the 'crises' were so interconnected that one of them could trigger a gigantic series of domino effects among the others. To realize this prompts a sense of frustration and of stupor, the same as one might feel when walking across a huge frozen lake covered with a layer of ever thinner ice. As we halt in our tracks, and realize open-mouthed how fragile our situation is, we hear all around us others yelling in unison: 'Go on! Run! Jump! Go faster! Don't stop!'

But beware: even if the news is catastrophic, we have to acknowledge that the global economic system – and a fortiori thermo-industrial civilization or even the entire Earth system – has still not collapsed. Indeed, the capitalist economic system is in the habit of feeding on crises to grow. This means that those who do not believe in a collapse can be told that there is still room for doubt. And it's true, there is indeed room for doubt (and there will continue to remain so for a long time, even after a collapse, but we will come back to this in chapter 6). All of this, then, raises many psychological, political and archaeological questions, which we will discuss in chapters 9 and 10. Before that, we need to deal with the question of time. It's fine to say that everything is going to collapse, but we still need to provide a few pointers as to how imminent such an event might be. After all, basically, all civilizations eventually collapse one day or another. How does this affect *us*, the present generations?

Part II

So, When's It Going to Happen?

6

The Difficulties of Being a Futurologist

So, when's it going to happen? 2020? 2030? 2100? Don't worry: we're not going to make a prognosis in this chapter. The difficulty, of course, lies in knowing what exactly we want to fix a date for. 'The collapse event' involves different time horizons. The rhythm of finance isn't the same as that of rising sea levels. The financiers are talking about an impending crisis because no lessons were learned from the 2008 crisis. Climatologists, meanwhile, deal both with current events and with what could happen in a few years or a few decades.

To try and find out what the future holds in store for us, we need to start out with certainties. We have seen that climate catastrophes are already occurring and will intensify. The same applies to the erosion of biodiversity, chemical pollution, wars for water and resources, major droughts, massive migrations, terrorist attacks, epidemics, financial crises, social tensions stemming from inequality, and so on. All this is a huge reservoir of potential disruptions (some very small) that can at any time unleash domino effects through the highly interconnected and locked-in structure of the world economic system. Scientists call these little sparks that can trigger an explosion 'femtorisks', in reference to the apparent insignificance of causes in comparison with their potential effects (femto- is a prefix meaning 10^{-15}).[1]

But how could we still believe in the urgency of the situation, given that disasters have been announced for more than forty years (actually since Malthus!). In the 1970s, many scientists tried to predict the future. Some were wrong, like Paul Ehrlich (in respect of a demographic prediction),[2] but others got it right, like Rachel Carson on the problems of using pesticides[3] and the meteorologist John S. Sawyer who, in an article published in the journal *Nature* in 1972, calculated the difference in temperature and the exact increase in CO_2 in the atmosphere for the period up to 2000.[4]

How can we still believe in all these tireless predictions? And who are we to believe? Warnings from the Club of Rome go back to 1972, and their model still remains valid (as we will see in chapter 8); and yet there are many who still do not believe it. Perhaps people are tired of apocalyptic warnings? Forty years waiting is a long time ...

However, the two eras are very different. Half a century ago, the Apocalypse took the form of a potential nuclear winter. The fear was real (and survivalist communities did appear) but ultimately nothing happened. Today, climatic and environmental catastrophes are less spectacular, but they have actually started. They cannot fail to take place.

On the other hand, if the possibility of industrial civilization collapsing is ever more palpable and real, we cannot be certain of its date. To predict the future, scientists build up their knowledge from dispersed data. From the millenarian prophecies of yesteryear to the contemporary fear of a nuclear winter, all the predictions of our societies' collapse have so far failed – everyone can see that no global collapse has occurred. So how can anyone be sure that we're not mistaken yet again? The answer is easy: we can't be sure. But there is evidence.

From risk assessment to intuition

To try to predict and avoid disasters or systemic shocks similar to 2008, some experts including insurers are developing tools for risk assessment and management. But 'the factors that determine the outcome and impact of invasions [...] are frequently complex and poorly understood'.[5] Femtorisks cannot be apprehended by traditional risk-management tools. Most societies clearly do not have adequate and sufficient resources to assess these risks.

If by chance all these risks can be identified, their evaluation and mitigation require a certain transparency and accountability on the part of institutions and decision makers. Now, this is increasingly difficult to obtain in highly complex systems because the unintended or unknown consequences of each person's individual actions increase considerably (this is also valid at the level of a state or an enterprise). This is the *moral hazard*: we behave as if we were not ourselves exposed to the risk. Some agents refuse to accept responsibility for their decisions but, more importantly, although their actions may be considered to be rational in normal times, they can lead to an inevitable collective failure.

Worse, there are insurmountable theoretical obstacles. Science does not have the tools to predict everything, and will never have them, as there are events that it is impossible to predict – the famous 'black swans'.[6] As the philosopher, mathematician and former trader Nassim Nicholas Taleb explains, classical methods of risk assessment are of little relevance to the forecasting of rare events or the behaviour of complex systems. Devised by Bertrand Russell and taken up by Taleb, the celebrated 'inductivist turkey problem' illustrates this perfectly. For turkeys on a turkey farm, everything is the best in the best of all possible worlds: the breeder comes every day to scatter grain for them, and the temperature is always comfortable. The turkeys live in a world of growth and abundance ... until Christmas Eve! If there were a turkey statistician specialized in risk management, on 23 December she would say to her fellow turkeys that they need have no worries for the future ...

The global economy survived the 2008 crisis. We can infer that the system is hyper-resilient, or that it has become considerably weaker, but we cannot prove that it will collapse or not collapse. According to one distinction made in 1921 by two economists, Knight and Keynes,[7] *risks* can be given a certain probability, whereas *uncertainty* can't. Uncertainty is the territory of the black swans; it is not quantifiable. You can't chart your way through it with Gauss curves and other risk-management tools. Moreover, confined within their disciplines, risk specialists see that 'for each of the risks they focus on, it is unlikely that the future holds a major tragedy in store for us'.[8]

Now, our society doesn't like uncertainty. It uses it as an obvious pretext for doing nothing, and society's functioning rests on its ability to predict future events. When this ability evaporates, we seem disoriented and lose the ability to come up with real projects.

So how are we to manage black swans? How are we to 'manage' the next 'Fukushima'? We cannot really do so. Instead, we need to let go and move from the 'observe, analyse, command and control' mode to a 'probe, act, sense, adjust' mode.[9] Open up reason to intuition. In collapsology, it is intuition – nurtured by solid knowledge

– which will be paramount. All the information contained in this book, however objective it might be, does not therefore constitute formal proof that a major collapse will take place soon, it merely allows you to increase your knowledge so you can refine your intuition and finally act with conviction.

The paradoxes of collapse

The reflections of the philosopher Jean-Pierre Dupuy are of great use in trying to understand the temporality of a collapse. After the attacks of 11 September 2001, something strange happened in the imaginations of people living in rich countries. Something clicked. 'The worst horror is now possible, as many people have been saying.' But, continues Dupuy, 'if it *is becoming* possible, it is because it was not possible before. And yet – so common sense (?) objects – if it has occurred, it *must have been* possible.' So we have experienced, as it were, an 'irruption of the possible into the impossible'. Before, it existed only in the minds of a few novelists. After, it has passed from the world of the imagination into the real world.

The philosopher Henri Bergson saw the same phenomenon in a work of art that, when it still does not exist, cannot be imaginable (otherwise it would have been created before). Thus the *possibility* of the artwork is created at the same time as the work. The time of catastrophes, explains Dupuy, involves this 'inverse temporality': the work, or the catastrophe, only becomes possible *retrospectively*. 'That's the source of our problem. If we are to forestall a catastrophe, we need to believe in its possibility before it happens.'[10] This paradox is, for Dupuy, the main obstacle (a conceptual obstacle) to a politics of catastrophe.

To solve this problem, Hans Jonas, in 1979, suggested that we listen more to prophecies of misfortune than to prophecies of happiness[11] in situations which have a catastrophic potential. In the same vein, Dupuy proposes a posture – which he calls enlightened catastrophism – to chart a way through the uncertainty of disasters. For him, increasing threats are not to be viewed as fateful probabilities or risks but as certainties. If we view them as certainties, we will be better able to avoid them. 'Unhappiness is our destiny, but it is a destiny only because human beings do not recognize in it the consequences of their own actions. Above all, it is a destiny we can choose to ward off.'[12] Collapse is certain, and that is why it is not tragic. For, in saying that, we have just opened the possibility of avoiding its catastrophic consequences.

There is another temporal curiosity mentioned by Bergson, namely the fact that after the occurrence of a catastrophic event, this is not experienced as catastrophic but as banal. And Dupuy comments:

> The terrible thing about a catastrophe is that not only do we not believe it will happen even though we have every reason to know that it will happen, but once it has happened, it appears to be part of the normal order of things. Its reality makes it banal. It was not considered possible before it actually occurred; after, it is integrated without further ado into the 'ontological furniture' of the world, to speak the jargon of the philosophers.[13]

So a collapse could become our new normal, thus gradually losing its exceptional, i.e., catastrophic character. From then on, there is every likelihood that we will be able to describe the collapse of our civilization only when it is far too late, through the work of historians or archaeologists.

And it is certain that these scholars will not agree on how to interpret this event.

One last paradox: if, conversely, we predict a collapse too early – i.e., now – and too authoritatively, for example through an official speech given by a head of state, it then becomes possible to instil panic into the markets (or the populations) and create a self-fulfilling prophecy. This then raises the following strategic question: can all of us together prepare for it without triggering it? Should we talk about it in public? Can we do so?

Beyond all these paradoxes and the impossibility of knowing with any certainty how many black swans exist, there are still some scientific tools that enable us to collect evidence about the nature of the future (and thus about the future of nature).

7

Can We Detect Warning Signs?

We have seen in chapter 3 that complex systems, and in particular ecosystems and the climate system, can suddenly tip over into another state in the manner of a switch to which a constant and increasing pressure is applied. The unpredictability of these shifts is enough to baffle any decision maker or strategic expert because, in our societies, choices are usually based on our ability to predict events. However, without a high degree of predictability, it is difficult to invest financially, humanely or technically in the right places and at the right time.

The crucial challenge is therefore to detect the warning signs of these catastrophic changes so as to anticipate them and react in time. More precisely, we need to learn to recognize the extreme fragility of a system that is approaching a tipping point, the very same one that paves the way for the 'little spark'. For example, in arid Mediterranean pastures, when vegetation shows irregular shapes in patches (in aerial views), this is because the ecosystem is not far from tipping over into a state of desertification that will be difficult to reverse.[1] This field of study, which investigates early warning signals, is a rapidly growing discipline.

The 'noise' of a system about to collapse

One of the most frequently observed characteristics of a system 'on the edge of the abyss' is that it takes longer to recover from a small disruption. Its recovery time after a shock lengthens – in other words, its resilience decreases. Researchers call this 'critical slowing down', identifiable by complex mathematical indices based on series of temporary data (autocorrelation, dissymmetry, variance, etc.) which reveal a system's state of fragility and therefore the possibility that it is about to reach a tipping point.

In the field, after the collapse of an ecosystem, researchers collect masses of data (environmental variables) that bear witness to past events, and analyse them. Some have even gone so far as to trigger experimentally – in the laboratory – collapses in populations so as to test these indicators. For instance, in 2010, two researchers from the Universities of Georgia and South Carolina exposed populations of *daphnia* (zooplankton) to increasingly damaged conditions (a reduction in food availability) and clearly observed warning signals of population collapse: a critical slowdown in population dynamics appeared up to eight generations before the population collapse.[2] Since then, similar findings have been observed for populations of yeast, cyanobacteria and aquatic ecosystems, but only in artificial and controlled conditions.[3] In 2014, a team of British climatologists was even able to identify the warning signals that preceded the collapse of the Atlantic Ocean current over the course of the last million years, an event that, if it took place today, would drastically change our climate.[4] But researchers still can't say precisely whether these signals are currently being produced.

New indicators are regularly added to the list of existing ones and increase the power of prediction of catastrophic changes. For the climate, for example, it has been observed that, at the end of a period of glaciation, temperature variations start going haywire and flickering before abruptly tipping over into a hot period.[5] This subtle index also works for lake ecosystems[6] but, although very reliable (it really does harbinger catastrophic changes), it only appears when it's too late to avoid such changes.

We cannot artificially disrupt a major ecosystem or a socio-ecological system for experimental purposes. So, researchers have so far contented themselves with observing natural or historical catastrophic changes without testing the predictions of these indicators in real life.

This method can nevertheless be used to classify systems according to the distance that separates them from a breakdown, i.e., according to their degree of resilience,[7] and this could prove to be very useful in making decisions, especially in biodiversity conservation policies.

In 2012, the discipline of warning signals benefited from major advances made by specialists in interaction networks, who are starting to clearly define the behaviour of very heterogeneous complex networks subjected to disruption.[8] For example, in a flowering meadow, imagine the immense web of relations between all species of pollinators (bees, flies, butterflies, etc.) and all pollinated plant species, where some species are specialists (in one flower) and others are generalists (they pollinate several species). This complex network of mutual interactions has a structure that makes it very resilient to disruptions (for example, the disappearance of some pollinators because of pesticides). On the other hand, observations, experiments and models show that these networks

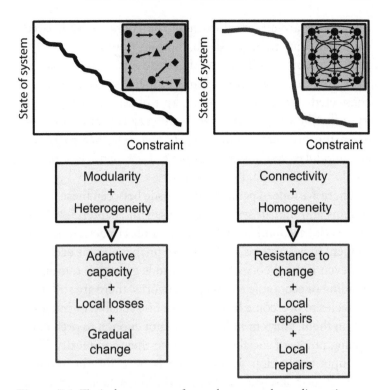

Figure 7.1 Typical responses of complex networks to disruptions

Source: after M. Scheffer et al., 'Anticipating Critical Transitions,' *Science* 338(6105), 2012: 344–8.

have hidden thresholds beyond which you must not venture on pain of seeing the network suddenly collapse.

More generally, it has been shown that complex networks are very sensitive to two factors: heterogeneity; and connectivity between their constituent elements[9] (see Figure 7.1). A heterogeneous and modular network (weakly connected, with independent parts) will withstand shocks by adapting. It will suffer only local losses and will gradually become more and more damaged. On the other hand, a homogeneous and highly connected network initially resists change because local losses are absorbed through the connectivity between elements. But, then, if the disruptions continue, it will be subject to domino effects and therefore catastrophic changes. In reality, the apparent resilience of these homogeneous and connected systems is misleading as it hides a growing fragility. Like the oak, these systems are very resistant but break when the pressure is too great. Conversely, heterogeneous and modular systems are resilient; they bend but do not break. Like the reed, they adapt.

There are indeed parallels to be made between these natural systems and human systems, as we saw in chapter 5.[10] These discoveries are fundamental when it comes to designing more resilient social systems, especially for finance and the economy. But even if the theory of networks adds greatly to our understanding of economic and social networks, there are still many obstacles to overcome before we can find reliable warning signals in them. Current indicators are not enough to predict the tipping points of social systems, given their complexity. Thus attempts to develop warning signals have for the moment failed, or no consensus on them has been reached.[11] Of course, we still have relevant indicators based on economic fundamentals when the situation is 'normal' but, as thresholds approach, it becomes impossible to evaluate anything. Some people have looked for critical slowing-down signs for financial systems but have not found any. Instead, they have found other indices that are not yet generalizable.[12] In short, for financial crises, the study of warning signals gives us a better grasp of how they work but does not make them any more predictable.

There will always be uncertainty

Science may make fantastic progress, but science will always come up against epistemological limits.[13] In this race against the clock we will always be running late,[14] as detecting a warning sign does not guarantee that the system has not already tipped over into another state.

To complicate matters further, warning signals may appear without being followed by a collapse and, conversely, collapses can arise without giving any warning signal. Sometimes, too, systems collapse 'gently', in a non-catastrophic way.[15] So we're dealing with a true 'biodiversity' of system collapse. This means that the best warning signals are *generalizable* but not universal: their presence is not synonymous with certainty but rather with a high probability of collapse.

Finally, and this is especially true for social and financial systems, it is very difficult and expensive to harvest good quality data in real time, and it is impossible to identify all the factors that contribute to the vulnerability of hyper-complex systems. It seems then that we are doomed, for the moment, to being able to take action only *after* catastrophes.[16]

For a complex system like the Earth system (see the study published in 2012 in the journal *Nature* and cited at the end of chapter 3), it is actually impossible, given our current knowledge, to state that the presence of global warning signals a collapse of 'Gaia' – and even less to give a date. But, thanks to these studies, we have gained the ability to 'possibilize' this catastrophe by referring to past geological events and by assuming there is a probability that this will happen.

But beware: the existence of uncertainty does not mean that the threat is any the less or that we have nothing to worry about. On the contrary, it is the main argument in favour of the enlightened catastrophist policy proposed by Jean-Pierre Dupuy: to act as if these abrupt changes were certain and so do everything to make sure they do not actually occur.

In fact, tools for predicting tipping points are very useful to show us that we have crossed boundaries (see chapter 3) and that we are entering a danger zone. Unfortunately, this very often means that it's already too late to hope for a return to an earlier, stable and known state. These tools allow us less to anticipate a specific date than to know what kind of future awaits us.

In collapsology, then, we need to accept the fact that we are not able to predict everything. This is a double-edged principle. On the one hand, we will never be able to say with any certainty that a general collapse is imminent (before having experienced it). In other words, sceptics will always be able to object on this basis. On the other hand, scientists will not be able to guarantee that we have not already seriously crossed certain boundaries, i.e., we cannot objectively assure humankind that the space in which it is living today is stable and safe. So there will always be grist to the pessimists' mill.

So what are we to do? Remember the 2009 earthquake in Aquila in Italy, when scientists were convicted by the courts for not having provided a clear estimate of the probabilities of a potential earthquake. The catastrophe happened in spite of the measuring instruments. Remember, too, the period leading up to the banking crisis of 2008, when some very insightful commentators sounded the alarm but were obviously not listened to. They were able *intuitively* to pick up many signs of an imminent crisis, such as speculative bubbles in the US real-estate market and the sudden increase in the price of gold that traditionally acts as a safe investment. But it was impossible for them to prove objectively and rationally what they were suggesting. The catastrophe happened without measuring instruments and in spite of the intuition of whistle-blowers. So how can we know? And who and what are we to believe?

Above all, not economic calculations or cost-benefit analyses – they're useless! Because 'as long as we are far from the thresholds, we can afford to mess with ecosystems with impunity'. There's no cost, it's all benefit! And as Dupuy points out, 'if we approach critical thresholds, the cost-benefit calculation becomes derisory. The only thing that matters then is not to cross them. [...] And we need to add that we don't even know where the thresholds are.'[17] Our ignorance, then, is not a question of the accumulation of scientific knowledge; it is consubstantial with the very nature of complex systems. In other words, in a time of uncertainty, it's intuition that counts.

8

What Do the Mathematical Models Say?

Another way to probe the future is to use mathematical and computer models. They do not enable us to predict the future but they give guidance on the behaviour and evolution of our systems and our societies. We have selected two models, one of which, HANDY, was developed in a study that created a stir at the start of 2014 because it was funded by NASA, and announced – according to the exaggerated remarks of some journalists – 'the imminent end of civilization'. The other, still valid after forty years of critiques and comparisons with real data, is the World3 model that served as a basis for the famous Meadows Report or Club of Rome Report.

An original model: HANDY

Developed by a multidisciplinary team composed of a mathematician, a sociologist and an ecologist, the HANDY model

(Human and Nature Dynamics) simulates the demographic dynamics of a fictional civilization subject to biophysical constraints.[1] It's a scientific experiment that aims to gain a better understanding of the phenomenon of collapse observed in the past and to explore the changes that would prevent it in the future. The originality of this new model lies in the fact that it incorporates the parameter of economic inequalities.

HANDY is based on a system of equations conceived in the 1920s by mathematicians Alfred Lokta and Vito Volterra, and frequently used in ecology to describe interactions between populations of predators and prey. In a schematic way, when prey is abundant, the population of predators thrives and causes a drop in the number of prey, and this in turn entails a collapse in the population of predators. The cycle then begins all over again since, when there are few predators, the number of prey again increases. Thus, in the long term, we have a kind of 'beat' in growths and declines, two sinusoids of population.

In the HANDY model, the predator is the human population and the prey is its environment. But unlike fish or wolves, humans possess this ability to extricate themselves from a Malthusian world where the limits of resources dictate the maximum size of the population. Thanks to their ability to create organized social groups, to use technology and to be able to produce and store surpluses, humans do not systematically suffer population decline at the slightest depletion of a natural resource. Thus two additional parameters have been introduced into the equations to make the model more realistic: the total amount of accumulated wealth; and the distribution of this between a small caste of 'elites' and a greater number of 'commoners'.

Three groups of scenarios have been explored. The first (a) assumes an egalitarian society in which there are no elites (elites = 0). The second (b) explores a fair society where there is an elite caste but where income from labour is distributed equitably between this caste of non-workers and the workers. Finally, the third (c) explores the possibilities of an inegalitarian society where elites appropriate the riches to the detriment of the commoners.

Before launching the simulations, the researchers vary the resource-consumption rates of each virtual society, generating four types of scenarios from the most sustainable to the most brutal: (1) populations slowly approach an equilibrium between population and environment; (2) the approach is uneven, showing an oscillatory motion before reaching an equilibrium; (3) cycles of growth and collapses; and (4) strong growth followed by an irreversible collapse.

In an egalitarian society without castes (a), when the consumption rate is not exaggerated, the society achieves an equilibrium (scenarios 1 and 2). When this rate increases, the society experiences cycles of growth and decline (3). And, finally, when consumption is sustained, the population grows before collapsing irreversibly (4). This first series of results shows that, regardless of inequalities, the rate of 'predation' of a society on natural resources is in itself a factor of collapse.

Now let's add the inequality parameter. In a 'fair' society, i.e., one where a small part of the population does not work but the majority does work and wealth is well distributed (b), a scenario of equilibrium can be achieved only if the level of consumption is low and growth is very slow. When consumption and growth accelerate, the society can tip over into the other three scenarios (disruptions, cycles of decline or collapse).

In an inegalitarian society where elites appropriate the wealth (c), which seems to correspond rather well to the reality of our world, the model indicates that a collapse is difficult to avoid, regardless of the consumption rate. However, there is a subtle difference. At a low rate of overall consumption, as one might expect, the caste of elites begins to grow and monopolizes a large amount of the resources available to the detriment of the commoners. These latter, weakened by poverty and hunger, are no longer able to provide enough work power to maintain the society, which thus starts to decline. It is therefore not the exhaustion of resources but the exhaustion of the people which causes the collapse of an inegalitarian society that is relatively modest in its consumption of resources. In other words, the population disappears faster than nature. According to researchers, the case of the Maya, where nature recovered after the collapse of the populations, follows this type of dynamic. So even if a society is overall 'sustainable', the overconsumption by a small elite leads irremediably to its decline.

In the case of an inegalitarian society that consumes a great deal of resources, the result is the same but the dynamic is the opposite: nature is exhausted faster than people, which makes the collapse swift and irreversible. This was typically the case for Easter Island or Mesopotamia, where the environment was still exhausted even after the disappearance of civilizations.

In general, what HANDY shows is that intense social stratification makes it difficult to avoid a collapse of civilization. The only way to avoid this outcome would therefore be to reduce economic inequalities within a population and to put in place measures that aim to keep the demographics below a critical level.

This model is an original attempt at modelling complex behaviour using a relatively simple mathematical structure – perhaps even a simplistic one, since you cannot model the world in four equations. However, this work is an important heuristic tool and indeed a warning which it would be wrong to dismiss out of hand.

In his book *How the Rich are Destroying the Earth*,[2] Hervé Kempf showed the close ties between inequality and consumption. The increase in economic disparities triggers an overall acceleration of consumption through a sociological phenomenon called 'conspicuous consumption', described for the first time by the sociologist Thorstein Veblen: every social class tends to do everything (and in particular to consume) so as to resemble the social class just above it. The poor strive to resemble the middle classes, and the latter seek to assume the attributes of the rich, who do everything to show that they are among the 'seriously rich'. This phenomenon is so powerful that consumption can, in rich societies, become inseparable from the construction of personal identity. Stuck in a model of competition, the society sinks into this infernal spiral of consumption and depletion of resources.

The HANDY model is all the more relevant as our society is currently displaying all the symptoms of the inegalitarian society that consumes a great deal of resources as described in the model. Since the 1980s, inequalities have exploded. The problem is that we now have evidence that economic inequalities are very toxic to our society.

According to Joseph Stiglitz, these inequalities discourage innovation and erode the confidence of whole populations by reinforcing a feeling of frustration that undermines people's trust in the political world and its institutions. 'Real democracy is more than the right to vote once every two or four years. [...] increasingly, and especially in the United States, it seems that the political system is more akin to "one dollar one vote" than to "one person one vote".'[3] Abstention is growing, but the stranglehold of the wealthiest (who *do* vote) on the way government works is increasing.

Inequalities are also toxic tor health. The feelings of anxiety, frustration, anger and injustice among those for whom such abundance lies beyond their grasp have a considerable impact on crime rate, life expectancy, psychiatric illnesses, child mortality, alcohol consumption, obesity rates, academic achievement and corporate violence. This finding has been remarkably well described, documented and costed by epidemiologists Richard Wilkinson and Kate Pickett in their bestseller *The Spirit Level*.[4] By comparing data from 23 industrialized countries (taking data from the United Nations and the World Bank), they discover that many of the health indicators of a country worsen not when its GDP drops but when the level of economic inequality rises. In other words, not only is economic inequality toxic to a society but equality is good for everyone, even for the rich!

Inequalities also generate economic and political instability. The two most important financial crises of the last hundred years – the Great Depression of 1929 and the stock market crash of 2008 – were both preceded by a sharp rise in inequality. According to the economic and financial journalist Stewart Lansley, the concentration of capital in the hands of a small elite caste leads not only to deflation but also to speculative bubbles, i.e., to a decline in economic resilience and therefore to intensified risks of financial collapse.[5] Repeated shocks erode confidence and especially growth in GDP, which only increases the disparities between classes. Worse, economic inequalities are also amplified by the adverse effects of climate change as these hit the poorest people and countries the hardest.[6] This negative spiral of inequalities cannot fail but lead finally to self-destruction.

For economist Thomas Piketty, it is the very structure of capitalism, its 'DNA', which favours the growth of inequalities.[7] In a large-scale historical analysis based on available tax records since the eighteenth century, he and his team demolish the conventional wisdom that the revenues generated by

GDP growth benefit the entire population of a country. In reality, wealth is concentrated inexorably in the hands of a small caste of rentiers when the return on capital (r) is higher than economic growth (g). This is simply a mechanical process. The only way to avoid this pitfall is to set up powerful national and international institutions to redistribute income fairly. But for such outbreaks of democracy to occur, we need extraordinary conditions. However, over the twentieth century, these conditions were met only after the disasters of the two world wars and the Great Depression of the 1930s. The financial world needs to be on its knees, sufficiently weakened for it to be controlled by powerful institutions. And this is all the more difficult as these institutions have prospered, thanks to the periods of rapid growth that have followed conflicts (with reconstruction as a stimulus) – a situation that we do not find today.

From this perspective, the 'Thirty Glorious Years' of growth and welfare in France (1945–75) were a 'historical aberration',[8] and the return of inequality since the 1980s seems therefore to be just a return to normal. In the United States, for example, the level of inequality recently went back up to what it was in 1929.[9]

What is most disturbing about this narrative is that we are now observing the inexorable return of inequality, despite the evidence of its corrosive effects on societies and despite the lessons of history. Could it be an inevitable destiny? Are we perhaps doomed to wait for the next war or, failing that, a collapse of civilization? Why are the elites doing nothing, even though it is obvious that they too will suffer from these two catastrophic outcomes?

To answer this question, let's go back for a moment to the HANDY model. It is particularly interesting to note that in both scenarios of the collapse of inegalitarian societies (famine among the commoners or a collapse of nature), the elites, cushioned by their wealth, do not suffer *immediately* from the first effects of the decline. They do not feel the effects of a disaster until long after the majority of the population or long after irreversible destruction of ecosystems – in other words, too late. 'This buffer of wealth allows Elites to continue "business as usual" despite the impending catastrophe'.[10]

Moreover, while some members of society are sounding the alarm to indicate that the system is heading towards an imminent collapse and advocating structural social change, the elites and their supporters are blinded by the long and seemingly sustainable period that precedes a collapse and take this as an excuse to do nothing.

These two mechanisms (the buffer effect of wealth and the excuse of a past of abundance), added to the innumerable causes of lock-in that prevent sociotechnical transitions from occurring (see chapter 4), seem to explain why the collapses observed in history have been permitted to take place by elites who seemed unaware of the catastrophic trajectory of their society. According to the developers of the HANDY model, in the case of the Roman Empire and the Maya, this is particularly obvious.

Today, as most poor countries and the majority of people in rich countries suffer from astonishing levels of inequality and the destruction of their living conditions, ever more piercing cries of alarm rise into the media sky. But those who find this annoying inveigh against 'catastrophism', while others shoot the messengers, and nobody really cares. Since the 1970s and the famous Meadows Report up to the latest report from the IPCC, including the synthesis documents of the WWF, the United Nations and the FAO, the message is clearly the same, apart from just one detail: the verbs are no longer conjugated in the future tense but in the present.

A robust model: World3

The World3 model is more than forty years old. It has been described in the bestseller (over twelve million copies sold worldwide) *The Limits to Growth*, better known as the 'report to the Club of Rome'.[11] However, the main message of this last text has been very poorly understood all this time, both by those who think they agree with it and by those who disagree. What it said was: if we start from the principle that there are physical limits to our world (this is a basic assumption), then a widespread collapse of our thermo-industrial civilization will most likely take place during the first half of the twenty-first century.

In the late 1960s, the Club of Rome[12] asked researchers at the Massachusetts Institute of Technology to study the long-term evolution of the 'world' system. They included Jay Forrester, professor of systems dynamics, and his students, including Dennis and Donella Meadows. These were the early days of computer science, and they decided to design a systemic computer model (World3) to describe the interactions between the world's main parameters, the six most important of which were population, industrial production, service production, food production, pollution levels and non-renewable resources. Then they fed it into a computer.

The goal of the game was to introduce the real data of the world into the model and press 'Enter' to simulate the behaviour of this world-system over a hundred and fifty years. The first result, called the 'standard run' and viewed as the business-as-usual scenario, highlighted how our system was extremely unstable, and described a widespread collapse in the twenty-first century (see Figure 8.1). Between 2015 and 2025, the economy and agricultural production start to fall apart, and they collapse completely before the end of

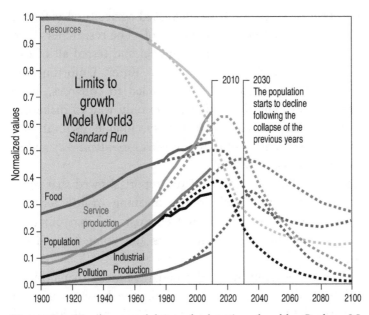

Figure 8.1 Meadows model, 'standard run', updated by Graham M. Turner.

Note: In bold, real data; dotted lines, the model.

Source: after Graham M. Turner, 'On the cusp of global collapse? Updated comparison of *The Limits to Growth* with historical data', *GAIA-Ecological Perspectives for Science and Society* 21(2), 2012: 116–24.

the century at a pace faster than the exponential growth that followed the Second World War. From 2030, the human population begins to decrease 'uncontrollably', finally sinking to about half of its maximum at the end of the century, about four billion people (these figures are approximate – they just give orders of magnitude).

Surprised by this result, the researchers then simulated 'solutions' in the form of as many scenarios as humankind could apply to try to make the system stable. What would happen if we developed efficient technologies? If we discovered new resources? If we stabilized population or industrial production? If we increased agricultural yields or if we brought pollution under control? The researchers then changed the parameters of the model and tested all of this in two or three clicks. Enter. Enter. Enter. Unfortunately, almost all the alternative scenarios led to collapses, some more catastrophic than others. The only way to make our 'world' stable – to end up with a 'sustainable' civilization – was to implement all of these measures *simultaneously* and to start as soon as the 1980s!

In the 1990s, an update of the report showed that these limits (and 'boundaries', in the meaning of the term as discussed in chapter 3) did indeed exist and that our civilization was approaching the limits and going beyond the boundaries.[13]

Even more definitively, the update showed that nothing had been done since 1972 to avoid the business-as-usual scenario.[14] On the contrary, since 1963, global industrial production had doubled every twenty-four years! In 2008, and then in 2012, an Australian scientist, Graham Turner, decided to compare the actual data over these last forty years with different scenarios to find out which one was closest to reality.[15] What was the result? Our world clearly behaved in accordance with the business-as-usual scenario – in other words, the worst scenario. And Turner concluded, 'This is a very clear alarm bell. We are not on a sustainable path.'

The model has not only resisted the innumerable and vehement criticisms aimed at it from the start but has even been corroborated by forty years' worth of facts. The main result of the Meadows Report is not that it predicts the future accurately, advocates 'zero growth' or announces that petrol will run out by 2000, as its detractors claimed. It simply warns us of the extreme instability of our system (as it generates exponentials). The model shows remarkably clearly how all crises are interconnected, as well as demonstrating the power of systemic thinking. We cannot be content with 'solving' just one problem, for example peak oil, or birth control, or pollution, as this would change almost nothing about the outcome. They must be tackled simultaneously.

After the 2004 version, the optimist on the team, Donella Meadows, liked to say that maybe there was a little window of opportunity not to be missed. The model indicated that three conditions would have to be met in order to maintain the economy and the population in equilibrium, given the Earth's carrying capacity.

Condition 1. If we can rapidly stabilize the population (an average of two children per family), then the population would reach 7.5 billion by 2040 (or 0.5 billion less than expected), which would make it possible to postpone for a few years a global collapse of the economy and the population. But that would not be enough. 'So we cannot prevent the collapse if we merely stabilize the world's population'; we need a second lever.

Condition 2. If we manage to stabilize global industrial production at 10 per cent above what it was in 2000 and redistribute the fruits of this production fairly, we would postpone the outcome by another few years. But that still would not be enough to avoid it because pollution levels would continue to rise and to jeopardize the regenerative capacities of ecosystems. So we need a third lever.

Condition 3. If greater technological efficiency is achieved, i.e., the levels of pollution and soil erosion are decreased while agricultural yields are increased, then the world could stabilize and allow a population of just below eight billion inhabitants to enjoy a good standard of living (close to the one we know) at the end of the twenty-first century. This scenario of equilibrium is possible only if the measures are implemented very quickly. But these results date back to 2004 ... It is impossible to advance any precise date but what is certain is that each year that goes by significantly reduces our room for manoeuvre.

The window of opportunity we might have used to avoid a global collapse is closing. So, on his European tour in 2011–12, Dennis Meadows, more pessimistic than ever, repeated in interviews and in an article he wrote for the Momentum Institute: 'It's too late for sustainable development, you have to prepare for shocks and urgently build small resilient systems.'[16]

So? What does your intuition suggest? 2020? 2030? 2100?

Part III

Collapsology

It's precisely because catastrophe is a hateful destiny which we must reject that we need to keep our eyes fixed on it, without ever losing sight of it.

Jean-Pierre Dupuy, *Pour un catastrophisme éclairé*

9

A Mosaic to Explore

In the first two parts of this book, we have shown that an imminent collapse of civilization is likely, and that this fate might even befall all of humankind, as well as part of the biosphere. However, it is not enough just to present the material bases and premonitory signs since this tells us nothing about *what a collapse might look like*. How could we add a little detail to this phenomenon so that we do not all start imagining it as a scene from *Mad Max*, *The Day After Tomorrow* or *World War Z*?

What are we talking about exactly?

It is precisely because the vocabulary relating to this subject is poor that the single word 'collapse' can 'explode' in different ways in each of our heads without leaving any room for a touch of subtlety. Like the Inuit, who are said to have about a hundred expressions to describe 'snow', we would have to invent a whole range of words to understand the complexity of the metamorphosis in civilization that awaits us.

From an etymological point of view, the French word for 'collapse' – *effondrement* – is instructive. It can refer to the action of breaking down something by smashing it (twelfth century), disembowelling an animal (fourteenth century), digging deep into the earth (eighteenth century) or collapsing (eighteenth); but it also designates suffering a fall in prices or a discouragement (both in the nineteenth century).[1] Today, it is used mainly to describe the collapse or the annihilation of a structure, an empire, shares on the stock market or the psychological state of a person.

In the community of historians and archaeologists, the word is used to describe the (relatively fast) *fall* or the (relatively slow) *decline* of kingdoms, empires, states, nations, societies and civilizations. The definition – largely accepted – provided by Jared Diamond describes it by the effects that it produces as 'a drastic decrease in human population size and/or political/economic/social complexity, over a considerable area, for an extended time'.[2] Yves Cochet's definition, quoted in the introduction, is perhaps less useful for archaeologists, but it is better adapted to our time: it is 'the process at the end of which basic needs (water, food, housing, clothing, energy, etc.) can no longer be provided [at a reasonable cost] to a majority of the population by services under legal supervision'.

The expression the 'collapse of industrial civilization' has a serious sound to it because it draws on three clichés. The first is that of a possible end to the great institutions guaranteeing law and social order: for a modern (and liberal) human being, this inevitably implies a return to barbarism. The second is that a collapse would be followed by a great void that it is hard to imagine, caught up as we are in the religious image of the Apocalypse. The third is that it seems to designate a relatively short moment, a brutal event, a guillotine clattering down on the whole of society that could easily be dated retrospectively.

According to some anthropological studies, an absence of governments or states does not necessarily imply a return to barbarism,[3] sometimes quite the opposite.[4] Also, collapses are not followed by the end of the world, as many examples from history demonstrate. Finally, they usually last several years, several decades or even centuries in the case of entire civilizations and are difficult to date precisely. So, in their prophetic essay *The Collapse of Western Civilization*,[5] the historians of science Naomi Oreskes and Erik Conway describe the collapse we are preparing ourselves to experience from the perspective of historians of the end of the twenty-first century. These historians decide to fix the beginning of the 'dark period' to 1988, when the IPCC was created. Indeed, didn't the sinking of the *Titanic* actually begin as soon as the alarm was sounded?

We have tried to use the word 'crisis' as little as possible as it creates the illusion that the situation is ephemeral. A crisis still fosters the hope that a return to normal is possible and therefore serves as a bogeyman that economic and political elites can brandish to subject the population to measures that would never have been tolerated 'in normal times'. By creating a sense of urgency, a crisis paradoxically boosts a sense of continuity.

It is interesting to note that the French vocabulary has only the word '*problème*' ('problem') to designate a very difficult situation (the synonyms for *problème* are weaker). Everyone knows that when you have a problem, you analyse the situation, you seek a *solution* (often of a technical kind) and you apply that solution, which makes the problem disappear. Like a crisis, a problem is one-off and reversible. But the English language has another word, 'predicament', which better describes the idea of collapse. A predicament is an inextricable, irreversible and complex situation for which there are no solutions, just measures for adapting to it. This is true of incurable diseases which, in the absence of 'solutions', oblige us to take paths – not always easy – that allow us to *live with* them.[6] Faced with a predicament, there are things we can do, but there are no solutions.

We did not use the term 'degrowth' because it designates less a historical reality than a voluntarist political programme (frugality and conviviality) intended, precisely, to *avoid* a collapse.[7] But this 'wish' gives us a glimpse of a gradual, controlled and voluntary reduction of our consumption of materials and energy – something which, as we shall see in the following pages, is not very realistic. Unlike degrowth, the notion of collapse still makes it possible to think of a future that is not totally mastered.

Often, the convergence of catastrophes is described with optimistic euphemisms that focus on what will succeed the modern industrial world. This is true of the 'metamorphosis' of Edgar Morin, the 'mutation' of Albert Jacquard and the 'transition' of Rob Hopkins. These expressions are very valuable for stirring enthusiasm among the crowds and helping us to imagine a future in ways that are not necessarily nihilistic or apocalyptic, but they too easily eliminate the sense of urgency and such questions as suffering, death, social tensions and geopolitical conflict. We will, however, happily use them in the framework of the 'politics of collapse', i.e., in cases where the factual description is no longer sufficient but where hope and a certain willpower are needed (see chapter 10).

What do past civilizations tell us ... ?

All the civilizations that preceded us, however powerful, suffered declines and collapses. Some may have picked up again, but others did not, and the reasons for which they declined have been vigorously debated for hundreds of years. The fourteenth-century Arab historian and philosopher Ibn Khaldun (1332–1406) is reputed to have been the first to articulate a coherent theory of the successive periods in the growth and decline of civilizations, in his famous work *Muqaddimah* (*Prolegomena*), written in 1377. In the eighteenth century, Montesquieu (1689–1755), in *Considerations on the Causes of the Grandeur and Decadence of the Romans*, and the British historian Edward Gibbon (1737–1794), in *Decline and Fall of the Roman Empire*, took a close interest in the greatness and decline of the Roman Empire. At the beginning of the twentieth century, following the archaeological discoveries of the previous century, Oswald Spengler (1880–1936), in *The Decline of the West*, and Arnold Toynbee (1889–1975), in *A Study of History*, also essayed 'universal histories' of civilizations which, although controversial in academic circles, greatly helped to make the subject popular. In France, from 1929 onwards, the *Annales* School paid particular attention to recurring elements and the constants of the past, using multifactorial approaches and an interdisciplinary method. Today, bestselling authors such as Jared Diamond, Joseph Tainter, Peter Turchin[8] and Bryan Ward-Perkins[9] testify to the diversity of points of view, hypotheses and interpretations that this topic generates but most agree, probably out of 'scholarly caution', that this historical and archaeological knowledge cannot be used to deduce anything about a possible collapse of our civilization. We will try, in this section, to be a little less cautious ...

The causes of collapse are usually grouped into two categories: endogenous causes, generated by society itself, instabilities of an economic, political or social order; and exogenous causes, related to external catastrophic events such as an abrupt climate change, an earthquake, a tsunami or a foreign invasion.

Jared Diamond has identified five recurrent and often synergistic factors of collapse in the societies he has studied: environmental damage or the depletion of resources; climate change; wars; the sudden loss of trading partners; and the (wrong-headed) reactions of a society to environmental problems. For him, ecological conditions are the main factor behind the collapse of the great Mayan cities at the dawn of the ninth century, the Vikings in the eleventh century, and Easter Island in the eighteenth century. But it would be wrong to reduce these ecological causes to mere external factors since, as he points out (and he is not the only one to do so), the only common factor behind all collapses is actually the fifth, that of sociopolitical order: institutional dysfunctions, ideological blindness, levels of inequality (see chapter 8), and above all the incapacity of a society – and especially its elites – to react appropriately to potentially catastrophic events. At the end of his book, Diamond ponders the reasons that push 'societies' to make bad decisions. He explains that human groups suffer from catastrophes for several reasons: they do not manage to foresee them; they do not perceive the causes behind them; they fail in their attempts to 'solve the problems'; or simply there are no relevant 'solutions', given the state of their knowledge.

In fact, this fifth factor increases the vulnerability of a society (its lack of resilience) and makes it highly sensitive to disruptions that it can normally cope with. This is what has recently prompted the archaeologist and geographer Karl W. Butzer to propose a new classification, distinguishing the 'preconditions' of a collapse (which make a society vulnerable) from 'triggers' (the shocks that can destabilize a society).[10] Preconditions are often endogenous (the incompetence or corruption of elites, a decrease in agricultural productivity, poverty, the depletion of natural resources, etc.); they reduce the resilience of a society and are factors of *decline*. Triggers, meanwhile, are faster and often exogenous (extreme weather events, invasions, the depletion of resources, economic crises, etc.)[11] and cause collapses if they are preceded by 'favourable' preconditions. In other words, what is usually called a 'natural' catastrophe is never really separate from human action.

Joseph Tainter extends this idea of a political dysfunction by adding a thermodynamic factor, noting that the growing complexity of sociopolitical institutions entails an ever higher 'metabolic cost' – growing needs for matter, energy and low entropy. In fact, the great civilizations are caught in an entropic trap from which it is almost impossible to escape. To use the words of the American political scientist William Ophuls, when 'the available energy and resources can no longer maintain the existing level of complexity, the civilization begins to consume itself by borrowing from the future and feeding off the past, thereby preparing the way for an eventual implosion'.[12] There follows a great period of 'simplification' in society, as was the case in Europe after the collapse of the Roman Empire, throughout the Middle Ages: less economic and professional specialization, less centralized control, less information flow between individuals and between groups, and less trade between territories.

Historians Peter Turchin and Sergey Nefedov have generalized this phenomenon by describing (and modelling) recent history as a succession of phases of surpluses and deficits in economic terms (and in energy!), i.e., in 'cycles' of structurally similar growth and decline. Mediaeval England (the Plantagenet cycle) and premodern England (the Tudor–Stuart cycle), mediaeval France (the Capetian cycle) and ancient Rome (the republican cycle), among others, have all gone through phases of expansion, stagflation, crises and decline.[13]

Historical and archaeological studies are constantly becoming more focused and detailed, witness Butzer's recent synthesis, which now allows us, thanks to a new heuristic framework, to deepen the study of the interactions between socio-economic and ecological dimensions rather than identifying just one or more factors responsible for collapse.[14] What lessons can we already draw from his findings?

... concerning the present?

Let us first note that the world is showing alarming signs with respect to at least three of the five factors identified by Diamond: environmental damage, climate change, and especially sociopolitical dysfunctions (a sociotechnical lock-in, the blindness of the elites, staggering levels of inequality, etc.). Thermo-industrial civilization, meanwhile, which concerns only a part of the world's population, *also* displays the characteristic signs of collapse identified by Tainter: an increasing complexity that consumes a huge amount of energy (chapter 5), coupled with the arrival of a phase of diminishing returns (chapter 2).

However, our situation differs from previous situations in three completely new ways: first of all, through the character of our industrial civilization and the threats hanging over it (climate, damage to the environment, lack of resources, systemic risks, etc.); secondly, through the simultaneous presence of several 'preconditions' and many potential 'triggers'; and finally through the potential interactions (and mutual reinforcements) between all these factors.[15] At present, the threats are therefore proportional to our power, and the 'height' from which we collapse could be measured by the yardstick of our extraordinary ability to stay 'above ground'.

How far are we sinking . . . ?

The answer is clear: we are sinking but not in any consistent fashion, either in time or in space. We will here present several models to try to grasp these dynamics.

The different stages of collapse

The Russian-American engineer Dmitry Orlov won fame by studying the collapse of the Soviet Union and comparing it to the collapse – imminent and inevitable, in his view – of the United States.[16] He recently proposed a new theoretical framework in which collapses can be broken down into five stages in order of increasing gravity[17]: financial, economic, political, social and cultural. At each stage, the collapse can stop there or deepen by going on to the next stage in a kind of spiral of collapse. The Soviet Union, for example, reached the third stage (political collapse), leading to considerable upheaval but not to the disappearance of Russian society. Orlov's scale provides us with a gradation for collapses which may be of different natures and intensity, similar to the Richter scale for earthquakes.

A *financial collapse* occurs when all 'faith in "business as usual" is lost. The future is no longer assumed to resemble the past in any way that allows risk to be assessed and financial assets to be guaranteed. Financial institutions become insolvent; savings are wiped out and access to capital is lost.'[18] So people have to wave goodbye to savings accounts, loans, investments, insurance and pensions! As happened in

Argentina in 2001, confidence, as well as the value of money, evaporates. Banks remain closed until further notice and the government implements emergency measures (nationalisations, quantitative easing, welfare, etc.) to try to avoid riots. In this case, suggests Orlov, it is better to learn to live with little or no money ...

A *commercial collapse* is triggered when 'faith that "the market shall provide" is lost. Money is devalued and/or becomes scarce, commodities are hoarded, import and retail chains break down and widespread shortages of survival necessities become the norm.'[19] The quantity and diversity of trade and information drastically decrease. The economy gradually 'decomplexifies'. As happened in Cuba in the 1990s, imports fall and shopping centres end up closing for lack of goods. Material abundance comes to an end and the informal economy explodes: barter, repair work of all kinds, recycling, flea markets, and so on. To master the course of events, the government attempts to regulate markets by imposing price controls or policies of rationing. In this case, it is better if you can provide for the basic needs of your family and community through your own means.

A *political collapse* occurs when 'faith that "the government will take care of you" is lost. As official attempts to mitigate widespread loss of access to commercial sources of survival necessities fail to make a difference, the political establishment loses legitimacy and relevance.'[20] This is a process of 'destructuring'. Proclaiming the need to maintain law and order, governments bring in curfews or martial law. As was the case in the former USSR, local corruption ends up running services formerly guaranteed by the administration. Public services are no longer provided, roads are no longer maintained, rubbish is largely left uncollected, and so on. According to Orlov, for the United States and the majority of rich countries, these first three stages are now inevitable.

A *social collapse* occurs when 'faith that "your people will take care of you" is lost, as local social institutions, be they charities or other groups that rush in to fill the power vacuum, run out of resources or fail through internal conflict'.[21] So we enter a world of clans and gangs, of civil wars and 'devil take the hindmost'. At this point, a process of 'depopulation' is triggered: conflict, displacement, malnutrition, famines, epidemics, etc. So it may be better to be part of small, still tightly knit communities in which trust and mutual aid are cardinal values.

A *cultural collapse* occurs when 'faith in the goodness of humanity is lost. People lose their capacity for "kindness, generosity, consideration, affection, honesty, hospitality, compassion, charity"'.[22] In this context, it becomes more and more difficult to identify with the other and, by losing that ability for empathy, we lose what is usually called 'our humanity'. Unfortunately, the humanities and social sciences have not really studied these exceptional situations.

More recently, Orlov suggested adding a sixth and last stage to this model, that of ecological collapse,[23] where the ability to reboot a society in an exhausted environment is very small, not to say impossible (see the end of this chapter).

Through time

The observation of socio-ecological systems (interactions between natural and human systems) shows that nothing that is alive is really stable or in a state of equilibrium. Complex systems tend to be subject to cyclical dynamics. According to the theory of the adaptive cycle (and of 'panarchy') developed by ecologists C. S. Holling and L. H. Gunderson as early as the 1970s as part of a study of ecological resilience,[24] all systems go through cycles of four phases: a phase of growth (r) where the system accumulates matter and energy;

a phase of conservation (K) where the system becomes more and more interconnected, rigid, and therefore vulnerable; a phase of collapse or 'loosening' (Ω); then a phase of rapid reorganization (α), leading to another phase of growth (in often very different conditions). The current industrial socio-economic system – if it can indeed be analysed by this model – would then have completed its phase of growth (chapter 1) and would be in a phase of conservation, characterized by increased vulnerability (chapters 2 and 3) and a rigidification of the system (chapter 4), due to a high degree of intercon-nectivity (chapter 5).

Moreover, and far from these cyclical patterns, there has been an attempt to study the dynamics specific to the phase of collapse in an attempt to answer the burning question: how long can it go on? For the physicist and analyst David Korowicz, this phase can theoretically follow three trajec-tories: a linear decline; an oscillating decline; or a systemic collapse.[25]

In the model of *linear decline*, economic phenomena respond proportionally to their causes. This is an unrealistic assumption where, for example, the relationship between oil consumption and GDP remains the same after peak oil. The economy would therefore decline gradually and in a con-trolled way, leaving us with the opportunity and especially the time to forge the basis for a great transition to renewable energy while radically changing our behaviour. This cor-responds to the most optimistic scenarios of the degrowth protestors and the 'transitioners' (see chapter 10).

According to the model of *oscillating decline*, the level of economic activity alternates between peaks of recovery and recession but with a general tendency to decline. There is a dynamics of this type in the case of the price of oil which, when high, plunges the economy into recession; this brings down the price of a barrel and thus allows for a semblance of growth to pick up until the price of a barrel reaches new heights. Every new recession damages the system's recovery capabilities a little more, and it gradually loses its resilience. Debts pile up and the possibility of investing in fossil fuels and renewable energies is reduced to zero. This model, similar (in its slowness) to the 'catabolic' collapse proposed by the futurist writer John Michael Greer,[26] is much more realistic than the first one and still leaves a sufficient margin for societies to adapt. It is currently our best hope and depends solely on the measures that we are *now implementing*.

Based on a much more precise study of the dynamics of complex systems and networks, the model of *systemic collapse* ascribes to our civilization the behaviour of a highly complex system, as we discussed in chapters 3 and 5.[27] But going beyond the invisible changeover points, combined with a succession of small disruptions, can cause changes the extent of which it is virtually impossible to anticipate. Causal relationships are non-linear, as the system is intertwined with many feedback loops. The consequence of this type of dynamics is that it is intellectually – and probably materially – difficult to envisage a gradual and controlled contraction of the overall economic system while maintaining the level of life necessary to control it. In other words, this model predicts that thresholds will be crossed in ways initially unnoticed but with subsequent effects that are cumulative, non-linear and brutal, rather than peaceful oscillations or a tranquil and controlled decline in the current economic system.

Through space

The heart of our industrial civilization comprises highly technical and complex societies where the peasant class has been reduced to a small percentage of the population and where many types of know-how and traditional sociabilities have disappeared. This is true of all the industrialized countries, with the exception of certain regions where 'progress' seems to have been neglected. Thus some 'remote' parts of eastern and southern Europe, or of Latin America, which still retain a peasant class are in what is known as the semi-periphery – an area where the influence of the world-system[28] is not yet total. That still leaves, on the periphery of the 'modern' world, a few areas that have been more or less spared, 'developing' areas that have retained a large part of their communal and traditional systems. They have 'maintained [...] ways of acting collectively to a remarkable degree'[29] for three reasons: they have remained small; they have kept themselves at a distance from the considerations of the states at the 'centre'; and they are remarkably creative when it comes to maintaining their fundamental values. The fall of a civilization or an empire is characterized first and foremost by its loss of control of the periphery, which reduces the resources available for the heart of the empire; this precipitates its fall.

This concentric description of the world appears useful if we remember that the 'heart' of the industrial world is the area that will suffer the most serious consequences of a collapse. For example, communities practising agroecology in Zambia or Malawi were scarcely affected by the food shortages caused by the economic crisis of 2008 because they were not connected to the global industrial system.[30] There were no hunger riots. European countries, meanwhile, have very little autonomy when it comes to their diet. In the United Kingdom, for example, it is estimated that arable land production accounts for only 50 per cent of the population's food needs.[31]

The possibility of a collapse occurring thus menaces the entire order of the world. The peripheral and semi-peripheral regions of the modern world-system are the most resilient, not only because the economic and energy crises they will suffer will be less grave (though not, of course, the crises due to climate change!) but mainly because they constitute a space of autonomy essential to the creation of systemic alternatives, a dynamic space of social change. So will the 'reboot centres' of a civilization be the regions currently viewed as the least 'advanced'?

... up to our necks?

Will we be able to restart the system after a short failure?

Who has not already imagined dropping everything, wiping the slate clean and starting over on a new basis? For the financial system, what could be more sensible than considering this possibility? But for the economic system, its industrial infrastructure and its production lines, this could be much more problematic for one simple reason: 'systems [...] shrink and decay'.[32] It is not so easy to restart. In the crash of 2008, for example, Germany suffered a sharp decrease in its transport activity. So trains and locomotives were temporarily shut down and when a year later the decision was made to restart them, many elements had suffered from damage that required significant and costly repairs.[33]

Our societies are resilient to the point of being able to handle sudden and relatively short interruptions (in food supplies, energy, transport, etc.). But the interruptions that last too long (from several days to several weeks) become irreversible once the entropic decomposition of production infrastructure becomes too significant. As in a heart attack, every minute counts and takes us further away from a potential 'return to normal'.

This 'reboot' effect is especially striking in that an emergency situation compels those present to focus their efforts on immediate needs and thus to sacrifice investments for the future. In addition, a succession of emergencies gradually reduces the adaptive capacity (resilience) of institutions and people, making them less and less able to organize 'reboots'. Populations would become poorer and more vulnerable and would no longer be able to rely on 'safety nets', such as insurance policies, to absorb the cost of catastrophes or on a globalized economy to redistribute food production. The more 'crises' and disasters there are, the less possible it will be to easily reboot 'the machine'.

More dramatic still, power outages that last too long, coupled with interruptions in the supply of oil, could interfere with the emergency shutdown procedures of nuclear reactors. Because – as we hardly need remind you – it takes weeks or even months of work, energy and maintenance to cool and shut down most reactors ...

Will it be possible to restart a civilization after a collapse?

Our civilization, that hyper-complex system, has enabled us to accumulate a gigantic amount of knowledge; this was possible because of the consumption of a large amount of energy (as we have seen) but also by networking a very large number of people. Indeed, anthropologists have long been aware that the complexity of a culture is proportional to the size of the human 'group' in which it developed. According to the theory, recently supported by an experiment carried out by a team of researchers from the University of Montpellier,[34] the bigger the groups, the less knowledge is lost accidentally and the more innovation thrives. In other words, large societies confer concrete evolutionary benefits in terms of adaptation to environmental conditions. But this advantage comes with a downside: you cannot go back. 'The more [...] we depend for our survival on large bodies of culturally transmitted knowledge, the more we rely on living in large groups.'[35] As the researchers note, reducing the size of a group can therefore entail significant losses in the skills base, and therefore accelerate a decline or trigger the collapse of a society. So the possibility that our industrial civilization may suffer 'deglobalization' and a 'reduction in complexity' comes with another risk: the impossibility of preserving the whole culture of our civilization, in which we find certain kinds of knowledge specific to the survival of a majority of us.

If it is not possible to transmit all of our knowledge to future generations, another major and recurrent problem arises: the nuclear risk. How are we to ensure that future generations can 'manage' this energy sector? Even now, this sector is facing a dramatic issue with regards to the renewal of knowledge. In France, for example:

> the CEO of EDF declared in 2011 that, by 2017, half of the people working in the nuclear industry would have retired. How can one train half of the technicians in a fleet of fifty-eight nuclear reactors in six years? [...] Many fresh graduates in nuclear engineering don't go into the industry, or leave it after a short time.[36]

More ironically, American researchers have realized that the best way to transmit knowledge over very long periods is the oral tradition, that is to say, the transmission of myths by speech (and not in writing or, even worse, via electronic data). So nuclear experts have sought advice from the 'specialists' of these traditions: the few North American Indians who are still alive, precisely those whose people were driven out to make way for uranium mining ...[37]

Without the technical knowledge already accumulated, how will future generations attempt to deal with the toxicity of the waste that our generation has produced? That is one crucial question that arises *only in the best of cases*, where the 230 or so reactors currently in operation have been successfully shut down. Indeed, not only do geopolitical instabilities and global heating seriously threaten the normal functioning of reactors (terrorism, armed conflicts, lack of water for cooling, flooding, etc.),[38] but if there should be a financial, economic and then political collapse of nuclearized regions, who will guarantee that the hundreds of technicians and engineers charged solely with shutting down the reactors will be kept in post?[39]

Of course, life does not stop after a nuclear accident, as evidenced by the return of wildlife to the region around the Chernobyl power station and especially in the ghost town of Pripyat. But what kind of life are we talking about here? Will it allow our descendants to rebuild a civilization?

10

And Where Do Human Beings Fit into All This?

At bottom, the real question posed by the collapse of industrial civilization, apart from its precise date, duration and speed, is mainly whether we, as individuals, will suffer or die in advance. Projected to the level of whole societies, this is the question of the potential durability of our descendants and even of our 'culture'. Might it all grind to a halt sooner than expected?

Collapse, and even the study of collapse, are opportunities to see human beings from another angle. So we will enter into the subject's mysteries through several doors: demography, psychology, sociology and politics, all of which are the branches of a still nascent collapsology.

How many of us will there be at the end of the century? The demography of collapse

We can't discuss collapse without addressing the demographic issue. The problem is that it is not possible to discuss demographics calmly. It's an absolutely taboo subject, and few are those who dare to approach the question publicly[1] for fear of rapidly arriving at a Godwin point (a moment after which any discussion becomes impossible because one person calls the other a Nazi). In demographics, this threshold is of another nature, but it's always the same: 'You want to do what they do in China, is that it?'

In a debate about the future of the world, you can approach all topics and discuss all the figures relating to energy, climate, agriculture, economy – but you can never call into question the official UN population figures: nine billion in 2050, and between ten and twelve billion in 2100.[2] Try it yourself: start, for example, a debate on the future of agriculture with anyone at all, and any discussion will begin with this mass number: nine billion in 2050.

Now – as it hardly needs to be said – this figure is a mathematical forecast that draws on a theoretical model. This model, moreover, is seriously disconnected from the realities of the Earth system as it is based solely on projected birth, mortality and immigration rates among current populations, without taking into account factors such as resources, energy, environment and pollution. It is therefore an approximate model, one that can be summarized as follows: our population is expected to reach nine billion in 2050, *all things being equal*. The problem is that all things do *not* remain equal, as we showed in the first part of this book. So it is possible that there will be fewer of us in 2050 or in 2100. If so, how many of us *will* there be?

For the Meadows team (see chapter 8), who developed a model at MIT much more closely based on the Earth system, the instability of our industrial civilization is leading to an 'irreversible and uncontrolled' decline in the human population after 2030. Of course, this is not a forecast – despite its robustness, this model does not take into account black swans, i.e., potential positive factors (brilliant inventions or advances in humanity) and potential negative factors (total war, a giant asteroid, serious nuclear accidents, etc.). So who are we to believe?

Cornucopians or Malthusians?

In fact, the significance of these two models is not so much that they provide us with good forecasts but that they shed light on two ways of seeing the world: the cornucopian vision and the Malthusian vision. The cornucopian person lives in the myth of the cornucopia or horn of abundance: the future is seen as a continuous and unlimited progress where human beings will continue to control their environment, thanks to their technical power and inventiveness. For the Malthusians, on the other hand, this power and inventiveness have limits (and thus boundaries), and it is now becoming difficult, not to say impossible, to continue along the path of continuous growth (of our consumption, our impact and our demographics) that we have been following since the beginnings of modernity.

These two imaginaries are neither incompatible nor exclusive. The one simply succeeds the other. Animals live in a Malthusian world where the limits of their population and their consumption are fixed by the ability of the environment to support them. Humans alternate between cornucopian and Malthusian phases, linking together cycles of civilizations over thousands of years: birth, growth, stagnation, decline, then renaissance or extinction. The growth phase is obviously cornucopian, as the environment is still relatively intact. Then, at each 'demographic surge', the noose of environmental limits tightens around the population; this stimulates technical innovation and makes it possible to artificially push back the initial physical limits.[3]

But there comes a time when civilization comes up against so many limits and boundaries (in general, climate, resources, complexity and politics) that it again brutally relapses into a Malthusian world. So population numbers fall because society is no longer able to maintain the conditions of its own survival.

So the question is whether (and when) the industrialized countries will relapse into this Malthusian world to join the procession of countries that are already suffering wars, famines and diseases. The overall mortality rate would then start to seriously rise again, curiously followed, a few years later, by the birth rate (but to a lesser extent). Indeed, the paradox is that, in a Malthusian world, human beings make a lot of babies! In a world of material abundance, however, birth rates fall (this is the famous 'demographic transition'). But the rising birth rate that would follow a collapse, the 'life force', could not compensate for the explosion of the mortality rate. On the contrary, it would contribute to an acceleration in the depletion of resources. Such would be the logic of a demographics of collapse.

These trends are described by the graphs in the Meadows Report but they need much more detailed and rigorous work. Meanwhile, the predictions of some collapsologists, based essentially on intuition or rough and ready calculations, continue to be churned out. They produce numbers ranging from a few million to one or two billion inhabitants on Earth in 2100 ... For if we consider the influx of fossil fuels that made the demographic explosion of the last century possible, it is very disturbing to imagine a world deprived, for example, of industrial nitrogen fertilizers (made from large quantities of natural gas).[4] For Vaclav Smil, a researcher specialized in the links between energy, environment and population, were it not for the fertilizers that allowed industrial agriculture to be highly productive (at a prohibitive cost in energy), two out of five people would not be alive in the world today.[5] In Belgium, for example, the fourth most densely populated country in the world, with nine inhabitants per hectare of arable land, one may wonder how the population will be fed if the industrial food system collapses before resilient and productive agro-ecological systems are set up.[6]

Should the population be wealthy or large?

People allergic to the debate on the declining birth rate argue that the ecological footprint must first be reduced per capita of the richest countries – and above all, that there should be a better distribution of wealth – before demographics is discussed. The argument is admissible, in so far as the impact of a population on its environment depends on three factors: its population (P), its standard of living (A) and its technological level (T) $[I = P \times A \times T]$.[7] But counting solely on a reduction in the last two terms (a reduction in the level of consumption and an increase in technological efficiency) is far from being enough to significantly affect our exponential trajectory. Not only have we never managed this (among other reasons because of the rebound effect[8] and the phenomenon of ostentatious consumption), but all these efforts will be in vain if the first term continues to increase.

The question of limits and the crossing of boundaries has become very awkward: while we wait for hypothetical political measures to reduce the unacceptable inequalities of our world, this question translates into demographic terms such as this: do we prefer overall to be fewer in number and to consume more, or to be more populous and to consume less? For now, the few attempts at a voluntary reduction in population and consumption have not produced very good results, and no serious institutional debates have as yet been initiated. But if we cannot at present decide collectively on who will be born (and in what numbers), will we be able in a few years' time to calmly decide who will die (and how)?

Will we kill each other off?
The sociology of collapse

A 'walking dead' future

Massive displacement of populations and conflicts over access to resources have already begun. The war in Darfur was one of the first (or at least best known) of 'climate wars'.[9] According to Harald Welzer, a social psychologist and specialist in the links between the evolution of societies and violence, these conflicts tend to grow and multiply because, whatever the causes, human beings construct identity fictions and thus always find a justification for killing each other. Even if the root causes are lack of resources, population displacement, famine, disease and extreme weather events, armed conflict can take on the guise of religious conflict or wars of conviction.

Welzer shows how a society can slowly and imperceptibly push the limits of the tolerable so far as to undermine its peaceful and humanistic values, sinking into what it would have considered unacceptable a few years earlier. People will get used to extreme climate events, periods of famine and population displacements – indeed, they are already doing so. The inhabitants of wealthy nations will also quite probably get used to ever more aggressive policies towards migrants or other states, but above all they will be less and less moved by the sense of injustice felt by the populations affected by catastrophes. It is this gap that will pave the way for future conflicts.

According to the latest IPCC report, '[c]limate change can indirectly increase risks of violent conflicts in the form of civil war and inter-group violence by amplifying well-documented drivers of these conflicts such as poverty and economic shocks'.[10] In 2013, a study published in the journal *Science* confirmed this trend, drawing on historical data going back more than ten thousand years and covering forty-five conflicts worldwide, concluding that a rise in average temperature and a change in the rate of precipitation were systematically correlated with an increase in interpersonal violence and armed conflict.[11]

Of course, climate will not be the sole cause of future conflicts, and this simple correlation should not conceal the fact that sociopolitical and cultural complexity of the relationships between societies and individuals is also at work in this kind of dynamics.[12] However, even if scientists are not yet able to quantify this correlation between climate and violence with any certainty (is it possible to do so?), they have no doubt that environmental disasters (energy, water, climate, pollution, etc.) will be an obvious source of armed conflict and social instability, particularly in emerging countries.[13]

The convergence of 'crises' is also seriously worrying armies, governments and national agencies responsible for guaranteeing internal security. As international security expert Nafeez Mosaddeq Ahmed points out, the Pentagon, for example, expects catastrophes to arouse widespread anger towards governments and institutions in the next few years.[14] The latter are therefore allowing for a world of tension and uncertainties by preparing for an increase in the frequency of armed conflict, riots and terrorist attacks, and by monitoring their populations, including pacifist movements, as revealed by Edward Snowden on the NSA's worldwide monitoring programmes. But it is often this escalation in *presumed* violence that generates real violence ...

Mutual aid in times of disaster

What scares us in the idea of a great catastrophe is the disappearance of the social order in which we live. It is an extremely widespread belief that, without the order that prevails before the disaster, everything rapidly degenerates into chaos, panic, selfishness and the war of all against all. As surprising as it may seem, this almost never happens. After a catastrophe, i.e., an event that suspends normal activities and threatens or causes serious damage to a broad community,[15] most human beings behave in extraordinarily altruistic, calm and composed ways (though this definition excludes situations where there is no surprise effect, such as concentration camps, and the more complex situations of armed conflict). 'Decades of meticulous sociological research on behavior in disasters, from the bombings of World War II to floods, tornadoes, earthquakes, and storms across the continent and around the world, have demonstrated this.'[16] In these situations, some people even take insane risks to help people around them, whether these be friends, relatives or perfect strangers. Surprising as it may seem, the image of human beings as selfish and panic-stricken in times of disaster is not at all corroborated by the facts.

Remember the images of the hurricane that devastated New Orleans in 2005 in the United States: aerial views of hundreds of house roofs submerged in a vast expanse of murky water, survivors – for the most part black – struggling and calling for help on those same roofs, rescue boats carrying residents and armed soldiers supervising search efforts and first aid … Remember the comments in the media: robberies, looting, rapes and murders … chaos.

A few years later, we can say with certainty that our imaginary deceived us. The images of floods and armed soldiers were perfectly real, but this memory of the catastrophe, or more precisely the memory of *the social violence resulting from the catastrophe*, does not correspond to reality. It corresponds to a discourse cobbled together and peddled by the media without prior verification. The crimes they described never actually occurred! This is all the more serious since this lie led to thousands of police officers and armed, tense soldiers being dispatched to the scene ... and they *really* assaulted local people in distress and caused real violence, which the media then fed on to justify the myth of violence in times of catastrophe.

The sources of this misunderstanding included the mayor of the city, Ray Nagin, and the chief of police, Edward Compass, who, very soon after the tragedy, circulated rumours of crimes, theft and even child rape. Much later, journalists would discover that these rumours were not based on fact, thus leading the police chief to resign and to publicly declare, 'We don't have any substantiated rapes.'[17]

When looking at the testimonies of survivors of the attacks of 11 September 2001, the bombings in London, train derailments, plane crashes, gas explosions or hurricanes, they all converge on the fact that the overwhelming majority of those involved remain calm, help each other and get organized. In fact, individuals seek security first and foremost, so they're not inclined to violence and are unlikely to do wrong to their fellows. In sum, behaviour associated with competitiveness and aggression is set aside in a general upsurge of feeling where all 'I's instantly become 'we's with a force that nothing seems to stop. It's as if extraordinary conditions bring out extraordinary behaviour.[18]

Human communities contain formidable 'self-healing' capabilities. Invisible in normal times, these very powerful mechanisms of social cohesion allow a community to be reborn after a shock by recreating social structures that favour its survival in the new environment. The real problem is that the emergency plans currently in place always concentrate their efforts on the preservation of physical structures (buildings, institutions, etc.). But scientists are starting to understand that economic and social networks are more resilient than buildings. The buildings collapse but human resources remain.[19] Preparing for a catastrophe thus means weaving a web of connections around you.

At this stage of research into the 'sociology of catastrophes', the crucial question is whether one can compare a one-off catastrophe to a set of intense, repeated, large-scale catastrophes when they start to loom. Will 'community resilience' work in the same way over the duration of a collapse? We absolutely cannot count on it. We know that in time of war (especially civil war), social order sometimes breaks down so quickly that the most barbaric acts can be committed in the most 'normal' populations. Nevertheless – and this is at least one thing to celebrate – we know that at the epicentre of a one-off catastrophe *that is not predicted*, human beings possess this unsuspected ability, which is already considerable in itself.

Mutual aid and altruism on one side and competition and aggression on the other are two sides of the same coin: human nature. Their relative proportions in an individual or a society depend on numerous factors. Like some secret, age-old recipe, the ingredients of mutual aid, that fragile alchemy, remain subtle and complex. Today, behavioural sciences are discovering that cooperation within human groups can very quickly turn into competition. But the opposite is also true.[20] In addition, many studies and observations contradict the founding myth of our liberal society, which consists in believing that the wild state of nature follows the law of the strongest and the war of all against all.[21] This research field is one of the most exciting – and urgent – in collapsology.

Nobody can tell from what material the social fabric of collapse will be compounded, but it is certain that mutual aid will play a considerable, not to say paramount, role. Indeed, it seems obvious that individualism is a luxury that only a very energy-rich society can afford. Why should we help each other if we all have 'half a thousand energy slaves' at our disposal?[22] To put it another way, in times of energy shortage, there is a strong presumption that individualists will be the first to die. Groups able to demonstrate remarkable cooperative behaviour will have a better chance of surviving, as has been the case for the millions of years that separate us from our common ancestry with other primates.[23] Paradoxically, therefore, we will soon be entering the era of mutual aid.

The importance of watching films and reading novels

However, we mustn't be naive. Things will be much more complex than we imagine. Thinking about collapse means constantly taking the trouble to give up a homogeneous vision of things.

In a situation of repeated serious crises, nobody will have the same view of events and so nobody will react in the same way. First, initial representations of the event (even if it has an objective impact) generally differ from one individual to another, so that those involved may not be talking about the same thing. Worse, if there are several events, as is often the case in chain reactions (a collapse of the stock market, which degenerates into a food or energy crisis, etc.), those involved may not be dealing with the same 'problems'. Therefore, it is certain that in case of repeated catastrophes, the goals of each person will be very different: while some will be obsessed with returning to the previous order, others will focus on the sustainability of institutions, and still others will take advantage of the situation to change the social order. In addition to all this, it will be difficult to acquire reliable information on the development of the situation in real time.

In fact, almost everything will be played out on the ground of the imaginary, of our representations of the world. For example, it is likely that some readers still don't believe what we stated in our previous section on mutual aid in times of disaster because they are convinced that human beings are fundamentally selfish and violent if not supervised by laws. Others, maybe, still believe that when a catastrophe occurs, people behave irrationally, screaming, jostling and running in all directions.[24] This imaginary of the irrational crowd, which is not based on facts but is continually fed by the Hollywood film industry, so thoroughly imbues our subconscious that we take it for granted.

Transitional initiatives have remarkably clearly understood that the battle (and the effort we need to make) takes place in the field of the imagination and storytelling. Indeed, every culture and every generation tells itself its own story. Stories convey the interpretations of historical events, the legends and the myths that help us understand how our world is arranged and how it could be deliberately adjusted or transformed. Stories give birth to collective identities, thus forming communities that share common destinies.[25]

Today, the dominant cultural narratives speak of technology, human ingenuity without limits, competition and the law of the strongest as the only principle of life, or the implacable forward march of progress. But it is an autopoietic loop (one which keeps itself going): we become survivalists because we believe in the myth of barbarism but, by preparing for the worst, we create a fear in others that favours a climate of tension, suspicion and violence, which then justifies the myth. What the transition needs is to play on the stories and myths to reverse these spirals of violence, nihilism and pessimism.

What if, while looking catastrophe straight in the eye, we were able to tell ourselves beautiful stories?

We badly need new transformative stories to help us enter a great period of uncertainty, narratives that would tell of a generation's success in liberating itself from fossil fuels, thanks, for example, to mutual aid and cooperation. Working on the imaginary means precisely that: finding stories that stop us getting into a state of cognitive dissonance and denial. 'Let's decolonize the imaginary!' as the economist Serge Latouche puts it.[26] Write, tell, imagine, arouse feelings … there will be a lot of work for artists in the years to come.

Transitional initiatives and their transition tales[27] are a good example. Through films, raps, newspaper articles, the television news of the future, comics and animations, transitioners are inventing their own future, one in which they would like to live in twenty or thirty years' time. By imagining a better future (but without oil and with an unstable climate), transitional initiatives are thus freeing people from the toxic sense of helplessness so prevalent in the population. 'This work on the collective imaginary helps strengthen local resilience, because it insensibly acculturates the population to the prospect of a post-oil and post-growth future, one that will inevitably be more sober'.[28] These stories also allow non-experts (in climate, energy, etc.) to play a part in planning a common future, a vision in the implementation of which they will also take an active role.

The most important, not to say most urgent, task is to rebuild a strong and vibrant local social fabric so as to gradually establish a climate of trust – ultimately, a 'social capital' that can serve in case of catastrophe. So right now we need to get out and about and create collective 'practices',[29] those aptitudes for living together that our materialist and individualist society has methodically and conscientiously torn apart in recent decades. We are convinced that these social skills are our only genuine guarantee of resilience in times of catastrophe.

Why do most people not believe it will happen? The psychology of collapse

The Big One, the earthquake that will devastate California: we know it will happen one day, but most Californians ignore it as they go about their daily lives. Now imagine that you're a Californian and that earthquake detection devices indicate that the Big One will probably happen before 2020, and surely before 2030. How would you react? Would it change your life?

When told the truth, most people tend to become pessimistic and resigned, or they just totally reject the message. Many factors may explain this behaviour.

Cognitive barriers: see no evil

There is a great deal of research in this field. Half of the book by philosopher Clive Hamilton, *Requiem for a Species*,[30] discusses this question: why have we failed to respond to the threat posed by global heating?

One first set of reasons is cognitive. We are simply not equipped to perceive the dangers posed by systemic or long-term threats. Conversely, our brains are very effective at dealing with immediate problems. Over past millennia, the selection pressures exerted by the environment have fostered our sensitivity to concrete and visible hazards,[31] and so we respond to risks by listening to our instinctive emotions rather than by using our reason or our intuition. Daniel Gilbert, professor of psychology at Harvard University, sums it up with a joke: 'Many environmentalists say climate change is happening too fast. No, it's happening too slowly. It's not happening nearly quickly enough to get our attention.'[32] Certainly, a summary report by the IPCC causes us to secrete less adrenaline than the sight of a growling wolf approaching: 'this explains why we react fearfully to events that are (now) objectively harmless, such as seeing a tarantula in a glass box or climbing to the observation deck of a sky-scraper, but show little fear in the presence of genuinely dangerous objects like guns and cars.'[33]

Moreover, there is the effect of habituation that we discussed early. This is illustrated by the frog that leaps out when plunged directly into a pot of boiling water but, when immersed in cold water that is gradually heated, stays in it and thus dies. We are accustomed to a barrel of oil now costing more than a hundred dollars, while in the 1980s and 1990s it was only twenty dollars. Similarly, how many professional English fishermen realize that, with all their on-board technology, they now bring back only 6 per cent of what their ancestors in sailing boats caught 120 years ago, even after spending the same amount of time at sea?[34]

Myths also prevent us from seeing the reality of catastrophes. The obsession with economic growth in our modern societies is extremely powerful. As Dennis Meadows, one of the authors of the 1972 report of the Club of Rome, says:

> if you believe that the market is led by an 'invisible hand', if you think that technology has the magic ability to solve all the problems caused by physical shortage or if you imagine that a divine presence will come down to earth to save us all from our madness, you are still showing a complete indifference to the question of physical limits.[35]

In fact, because these myths founded our identity and our vision of the world and are deeply rooted in our minds, they simply cannot be challenged by every new piece of information that arrives. The opposite is true: the mind seeks every means of fitting new information into the framework of its founding myth.

Denial: believe no evil

The strangest and most fascinating aspect of the problematics of catastrophe is that it is not uncommon for us to know what's going on – and what might happen – but not to believe it. Indeed, no one these days can say that there is a lack of scientific data referring to alarming findings or that the media don't mention them frequently enough. But it is clear that, for most people, this information is not credible. 'We consider the catastrophe to be impossible at the very same time as the data at our disposal make it likely and even certain or almost certain. [...] It is not uncertainty, scientific or not, which is the obstacle, but the impossibility of believing that the worst will happen'.[36] In other words, the accumulation of scientific data is necessary but not sufficient to fully deal with the question of collapse.

As Dennis Meadows has observed, over the last forty years 'we simply continued to change the reasons for not changing our behaviour'.[37] As proof, he compares the reactions that his report has met with over the decades.

> In the 1970s, critics claimed, 'There are no limits. Anyone who thinks there are limits simply doesn't get it ...' In the 1980s, it became clear that the limits existed, so the critics then said, 'Okay, there are limits, but they're very far away. We don't need to worry.' In the 1990s, it became apparent that they weren't that far away. [...] So, supporters of the growth claimed, 'The limits may be close but we don't need to worry about them because markets and technology

will solve the problems.' In the 2000s it started to seem that technology and the market would not solve the question of limits. The answer changed once more: 'we must continue to support growth, because that's what will give us the resources we need to deal with the problems.'[38]

Clive Hamilton has analysed all the forms of denial that prevent us from facing the reality of global heating. One of the most important, in his view, is the phenomenon of cognitive dissonance, which he illustrates with the history of a cult that spread through the United States in the 1950s. The guru, a woman named Marian Keech, claimed to be receiving messages from an alien who told her that the Last Judgement was nigh. An apocalyptic flood would soon sweep over the human race and the extraterrestrial would send a space shuttle to rescue believers at midnight on 21 December 1954. On that day, the followers of the sect met, but no alien came to pick them up.

Contrary to what one might think, the reaction of members of the sect was neither disappointment nor despair – quite the contrary! They hurried to tell the press why they were so excited: the extraterrestrial had finally decided to save humankind, thanks to the light spread by the group of followers. So, in contrast to the sceptics who thought that everything the sect did was futile, Marian Keech, contrary to expectations, claimed that it was precisely the devotion of all its members that had saved humankind. Myth is stronger than facts.

For Meadows, it's clear that 'we don't want to know what's really going on, we want confirmation of a set of impressions we have already'.[39] Climate sceptics, for example, are not real sceptics; they are not looking for facts that they could submit to rigorous analysis. On the contrary, they oppose everything that contradicts their worldview and then look for reasons to justify this rejection.

They even went further, organizing a real collective enterprise of 'active' denial. Some very big players in the industrial world financed think tanks and managed to create a 'climate' of uncertainty and controversy around some perfectly well-established scientific facts. This strategy of doubt and ignorance, aimed at hiding the harmful effects of their products, is today well documented in the case of tobacco, asbestos, pesticides, endocrine disruptors and, more recently, global heating.[40] It was particularly effective in causing the failure of the 2009 climate negotiations in Copenhagen and was doubtless at work before and during the Paris Summit in December 2015.

But multinationals and oil companies are not the only culprits; governments too have their share of responsibility, as evidenced by the passing of a law in North Carolina which forbids anyone to speak in public about rising sea levels. Then there are the new laws on 'responsible management of state expenditure', so it is easy to understand the discomfiture of climatologists, who are losing the opportunity – and the right! – to discuss their results at scientific conferences or report them to the media.[41]

Are we being too catastrophist?

The psychology of collapse is full of contradictions and misunderstandings. Many complain that IPCC reports are too alarmist and that the media easily fall into the same vein. But we need to remember that the IPCC represents a consensus! It therefore generates – by definition – a consensual, neutral, watered-down discourse that contrasts with many scientific publications, and does not take into account the most recent studies (which are often the most catastrophist).[42] If we are to believe the facts, the IPCC is anything but pessimistic.

Moreover, while the catastrophist attitude is, in general, not popular, many people still think and *believe* that misfortunes may happen to them. Every time they sign an insurance contract, they betray this belief. Now, accidents – fires, flights, floods, etc. – are very or extremely rare in a lifetime, and few people are familiar with the scientific basis for calculating the risks of these events, which are intuitively considered as *possible* and thus trigger concrete actions, while the consequences of climate change, which are well supported by the facts, are ignored. In fact, the consequences of climate change 'have been systematically underestimated by both campaigners and, until very recently, most scientists'.[43] They were all worried about 'immobilizing the public with too much fear'.[44] So is there a threshold of catastrophism beyond which the mind would refuse to go? Is all this only a question of degree? Should we therefore avoid the language of catastrophe *at all costs*? More specifically, is the notorious absence of any concrete political results from political ecology over the last forty years due to an over-catastrophist discourse or, on the contrary, to an over-bland discourse?

Everyone will have their opinion on the matter but, in the meantime, the impasse is obvious: either we say things as they are, straightforwardly, and then run the risk of being called birds of ill omen and lose all credibility; or we sugar the pill, avoiding hard numbers (about the climate or any other environmental disaster), and then we run the risk of being relegated to the bottom drawer of political priorities because the situation is not yet considered to be all that serious.

In fact, experiments in social psychology have shown that, for people to take a threat seriously, they need to be well informed about the situation and to have credible, reliable and accessible alternatives.[45] If they have only partial information and can play only a limited role, people are less likely to commit. Thus one of the conditions for encouraging people to take action is to provide the most comprehensive information possible about catastrophes. The problem, in fact, stems from the other ingredient: there is really no alternative to a collapse (just means of adapting to it) and it is difficult to take any concrete, fast and accessible form of action.

See, believe ... and react!

Nevertheless, there are still people who can listen, understand and believe an article, a speech or a story about the collapse of our globalized society and even of the human species. In our own many public interventions and private conversations, we face various types of reactions from people who seem convinced that a collapse is imminent. We have classified them and here present a non-exhaustive list which (just this once) will not be based on bibliographic references but on a completely subjective experience. May future research in collapsology add a little rigour to this typology.

Theshitsgonnahitthefan reactions (or 'it's all kicking off') are common in people who feel helpless in the face of the destruction of our world and who, for this or for some other reason, have developed a certain resentment or even anger towards society. 'A collapse? Bring it on! This society is so rotten anyway ... Long live collapse, say I!' But apart from the fact that this attitude reveals a very dark and even nihilistic imaginary of catastrophe, it does not allow us to know precisely whether people are also imagining their own death, or whether they see themselves among the survivors, contemplating the decline of the city from the top of the hill overlooking it and savouring a well-deserved revenge. Needless to say, this attitude is relatively toxic for any political and social organization in times of catastrophe ...

Whatsthepoint reactions ('we're all doomed') are extremely frequent. The world's going to end so why keep killing yourself trying to avoid it? 'We're screwed anyway, so let's make the most of what time we have left!' But we need to be careful: in this kind of reaction, we can distinguish two trends that play on the ambiguity of the phrase 'make the most of it'. There is the likeable – but selfish – Rabelaisian and Epicurean tendency: those people who would spend the rest of their lives down the pub, having a laugh and savouring the last pleasures of life. And there are the 'bastards', who makes the most of things to the detriment of others. We grab the maximum allowance of petrol, we overconsume, and we ransack the place one last time before leaving.

Survivalists, or *preppers* ('we're all on our own'), are found more and more frequently throughout the world. Everyone must have seen a report or a documentary about these individuals who barricade themselves away, lock themselves up, bury themselves in bunkers and store impressive quantities of weapons and essential products. When they're not teaching archery to their children, they're practising how to recognize edible wild plants or learn water purification techniques. They are preparing for violence, believing that others (neighbours? invaders?) will react in the same way they will, probably violently. The imaginary that underlies this posture is fed by films such as *Mad Max* or zombie movies, and a belief that human beings are profoundly wicked. 'You travel faster when you travel alone' could be their motto.

The *transitioners* ('we're all in the same boat') are very often non-violent (they probably think they can't even *be* violent) and have a collectivist spirit. They call for a large-scale 'transition' because, for them, life no longer makes sense if the rest of the world collapses. So, rather than withdrawing from the world, they practise openness and inclusiveness, convinced that the future belongs to ecovillages, and they support mutual aid networks between transitional initiatives. 'You travel further when you travel together' could be their motto.

Collapsologists discover they have a passion for this subject, a subject that nobody talks about but that gives meaning to their lives. Studying, sharing, writing, communicating, understanding all gradually become time-consuming activities, which can be gauged by the frequency and length of the books published and the articles and comments posted on blogs and websites dedicated to this topic. Curiously, these 'geeks of collapse', the most famous of whom are nicknamed 'collapsniks', are often engineers ... and men. It is also, if we are to believe one veteran of the movement, a common factor in break-ups between couples because, while the woman views collapse as just one topic of conversation among others (and asks her husband not to broach this subject when at home with his family or in front of her women friends), the husband starts to get the bunker ready or to attend endless transitional meetings ... Clichés aside, the split between men and women is very evident in the non-specialist world, where men tend much more to discuss numbers, facts and technology (e.g., relating to energy) than women, who are happier to approach the emotional and spiritual aspects of the question (at least publicly).

In the real world, which is always much more complex, some people may feel they belong to several categories. For example, as a collapsologist, it is difficult not to engage in forecasting and even, like some people, to hope that a collapse might happen quickly so as to avoid too drastic climatic consequences (see the end of this chapter) and to practise harvesting wild edible plants, *while still being convinced* that cooperation is the only possible way out of the dilemma ...

But how are we to live with it?

In reality, denial is a salutary cognitive process (in the short term!), which helps us protect ourselves naturally from over-'toxic' information. Indeed, the possibility of a collapse often causes great anxiety, which is very harmful to the body if it becomes chronic. The absence of concrete alternatives even generates a feeling of impotence, which itself is carcinogenic[46] (but which disappears once we take action). But also, 'refusing to accept that we face a very unpleasant future becomes perverse'[47] to the extent that we underestimate the long-term effects of catastrophes. So what are we to do? How are we to stay in good health?

One initial response is to see any 'psychological transition' as a process of mourning. Climate disasters, or 'the possibility that the world as we know it is heading for a horrible end,'[48] are often too difficult for the human mind to accept. 'It's the same with our own deaths; we all "accept" that we will die, but it is only when death is imminent that we confront the true meaning of our mortality.'[49]

The grieving process goes through several stages, according to the well-known model established by Elisabeth Kübler-Ross, the American psychologist and specialist in mourning: denial, anger, bargaining, depression and acceptance. We find all these steps in the reactions of the public and even in the reactions we encountered while writing this book. In discussions and workshops on transition or collapse, we found that moments of witnessing, and the sharing of emotions, were essential to enable those present to realize that they were not alone in facing this kind of future and feeling these emotions. All these moments brought us closer to the acceptance stage, which is essential if we are to regain a sense of gratitude and hope which nourishes fair and effective action.

To forge ahead, to find a desirable future and to see collapse as a tremendous opportunity for society necessarily involves passing through unpleasant phases of despair, fear and anger. This forces us to dive deep into our personal shadow zones, to look them in the face and to learn to live with them. The 'work' of mourning is therefore both collective and personal. As the remarkable studies by Clive Hamilton, Joanna Macy, Bill Plotkin and Carolyn Baker show,[50] it is only by digging deep and sharing those emotions that we will regain the taste for action and find new meaning in our lives. This is neither more nor less than a symbolic passage to adulthood. Currently, mutual aid networks, quite discreet but powerful, are flourishing around the world, and growing at a speed equalled only by the happiness they provide.[51]

This shift can be liberating, as the philosopher Clive Hamilton says:

> On one level, I felt relief: relief at finally admitting what my rational brain had been telling me; relief at no longer having to spend energy on false hopes; and relief at being able to let go of some anger at the politicians, business executives and climate sceptics who are largely responsible for delaying action against global heating until it became too late.[52]

Finally, the process of mourning also involves a feeling of justice. People who suffer from a loss that they consider unfair must be able to punish possible culprits (or see them punished)[53] if they are to avoid an outburst of anger that may be expressed in the form of social violence or psychosomatic diseases. In the case of the collapse of our society, this is of particular concern. Indeed, a people that feels humiliated will easily express anger in some outward form, resorting to extreme violence, directed – wrongly – against scapegoats or those actually responsible for the injustice. The history books are filled with examples of this type. Today, the work of many historians, journalists and activists is shedding light on the responsibility that various people or organizations share in the advent of the catastrophes that we face. 'Our children will blame us,' as we often hear. Good luck to them! These children may already be old enough to sue us ...

Now that we believe in it, what shall we do? The politics of collapse

Constructive and, if possible, non-violent action can clearly come about only once we have gone through several psychological stages, individually and collectively. But let's be realistic, we can't reasonably afford to wait for everyone to start the mourning process before we take action. First, it's too late for that and, second, human beings don't work that way. In reality, action is not the culmination of a process but an integral part of the process of 'inner transition'. It is action which means that, *as soon as we have become aware of the situation*, we can emerge from an uncomfortable helplessness since action provides daily fulfilment that keeps us optimistic. These are at first small actions which may seem insignificant, but then become more intense as a consequence of the gratifications that everyone can draw from them. It is through acting that our imagination is transformed. And that's also why, depending on everyone's personal affinities and life stories, some people will choose the path of violent (and more or less emancipatory) insurrection, others will defend their identity or take flight, and still others will embark on building non-violent alternatives. The 'mosaic of collapse' will then occupy a full spectrum of possibilities.

Whatever stage we are at, we must continue to live, immersed in this 'world of yesterday', with all the contradictions and inertia that this implies. Each of us will therefore find opportunities to act *in the face of collapse*, depending on our affinities and the social environment in which we decide to live. The main thing, to begin with, is that a deep-seated belief in collapse should not make our present too unpleasant – for ourselves or for our friends and relatives – because we will need much emotional comfort to get through these troubled and uncertain times.

Transition: anticipation and resilience

Political movements that focus on the prospect of collapse are few and far between. The most constructive and pacifist of them (we will not here discuss the insurrectional movements)[54] are those of transition and degrowth.

In general, human beings do not believe in the eventuality of a catastrophe until it has actually happened, i.e., too late. The principle of *transition* and *degrowth* attempts precisely to overcome this problem by foreseeing catastrophes. Anticipating the end of fossil fuels, severe climate change and disruptions in food supply are all examples of the programme put forward by the 'transitioners' and degrowth protestors (who are often probably the same people). Because even if it is too late to build a true steady-state economy, it is never too late to build small-scale local resilient systems better able to endure the coming economic, social and ecological shocks.

Although small and inevitably local, these initiatives are spreading at an amazing pace. The transition initiatives movement (formerly known as 'Cities in Transition'), initiated in Great Britain in 2006, has in less than ten years carried out several thousand experiments on the five continents. This movement, which met with a great deal of enthusiasm, is already having a tangible impact on the lives of those involved: citizens' cooperatives for renewable energy, local and sustainable food systems (urban agriculture, permaculture, community-supported agriculture) and new cooperative economic models, and so on. There is no lack of examples. To find them, just read a few newspapers,[55] open one of the countless books dedicated to 'concrete' and 'positive'[56] alternatives, or spend an hour on the internet.

From a political point of view, transition is a strange and paradoxical thing. It involves both accepting the imminence of catastrophes – i.e., saying goodbye to our industrial civilization – and fostering the emergence of new small, low-tech systems that do not yet constitute a 'model' or a 'system'. From a concrete point of view, the transition phase – temporary by definition – must therefore enable two systems to coexist, one dying and the other being born, inconsistent on many points in their objectives and strategies (e.g., on growth: see chapter 4).

As for the posture, it is *both* catastrophist and optimistic, that is to say, both lucid and pragmatic. Lucid, because the people involved in these movements are not in denial about catastrophes. Most of them have given up the myth of eternal growth as well as the myth of the Apocalypse. They know *and believe in* what awaits us, and are generally receptive to catastrophist language because they already are committed to the search for real alternatives. Pragmatic because 'catastrophist political thinking is not apocalyptic in nature: it does not claim to be worried about the end of the world but more precisely about a sudden and potentially traumatic reorganization of ecosystems and societies.'[57] Neither business as usual nor the end of the world: just a world to invent, together, here and now.

It also takes a good dose of willpower, a bit of chutzpah and a hint of naivety. Indeed, the success of the transition movement stems from the fact that its participants have a 'positive vision' of the future. To avoid sinking into the doldrums, they imagine (together) a future in which, by 2030, there will be no oil and the climate will be unpredictable, but it will still be good to live! The power of the imagination lies in the details. Just sketch them out, imagine them, dream them together ... then roll up your sleeves and start making them real. This strategy has proved extremely powerful in terms of mobilization and creativity.[58]

Generalizing this 'paradoxical' policy raises another problem: the fact that it is necessary to accept, publicly and officially, the death of the old world. Making it official mainly means running the risk of self-fulfilling prophecies (see chapter 6): as soon as a prime minister declares that he is preparing the country for a collapse, stock markets and populations will react with a certain nervousness ... causing disruptions that will only accelerate the occurrence of just what the prime minister was trying to stave off.

A transition policy is therefore necessarily 'dialogic', as Edgar Morin put it – woven from paradoxes such as 'death/life' (it is the death of our industrial society that will allow the emergence of new forms of society) and 'continuity/break' (we need *simultaneously* to foresee medium-term transition policies and catastrophic disruptive events).

At the level of territory, the leitmotif of transition is the need to create 'local resilience',[59] that is, to increase the capacity of local communities to recover from very diverse systemic disruptions (food, energy, social order, climate, etc.). At the macroeconomic level, we will need to invent an economy of 'energy descent' – or degrowth – no longer based on a debt system but on other much more sensible paradigms, such as choosing a more modest lifestyle, sharing things fairly or, why not, rationing (a mixture of these).

These huge projects are in their infancy,[60] and their success is uncertain. Indeed, not only is it very difficult to transform our economic system in a flexible and voluntary way without economic growth (see chapter 4), but it is not normally possible for a society to voluntarily reduce its consumption in the long term. Historical examples of societies that knew how to limit themselves so as to avoid a collapse are extremely rare. The best-known example is the tiny pacific island of Tikopia, cited by Jared Diamond,[61] where the inhabitants have survived for more than three thousand years at the limits of the carrying capacity of their island, thanks to devoted tree cultivation and stringent birth-control policies.

However, and it is exciting to see this, as soon as the first economic and social shocks appear, alternatives emerge very quickly, witness the protest/creation movements that are spreading across Greece, Portugal and Spain[62] and foreshadow the world of tomorrow.

Finally, the concept of transition brings people and things together. It does not radically disrupt the imaginary of continuous progress, but it allows a catastrophist lucidity to flourish. It enables us to find common practices and shared positive imaginaries, which is in itself remarkable. Transitioners do not wait for governments; they are already inventing ways of living through this collapse in a non-tragic way. They are not waiting for the worst but building the best.

The politics of the big disconnect

The transition could finally be seen as an act of 'disconnection'. Disconnecting from the industrial system involves giving up *in advance* everything it provides us with (industrial food, clothes, rapid travel, various objects, electronic implements, etc.) before being forced to undergo shortages. But for many people, disconnecting quickly and by yourself means dying. Indeed, few of the inhabitants of rich countries know how to eat, how to build a house, get dressed or move without the help of the industrial system. The challenge lies in organizing, rediscovering the knowledge and techniques that allow us to regain possession of our livelihood *before* we disconnect. The paths towards autonomy are then necessarily collective since without fossil fuels the amount of work to be done to try to compensate for their lack will be considerable (a barrel of oil equals about 24,000 hours of human work, i.e., eleven years at a rate of 40 hours a week).[63] Once 'connected' to smaller, more resilient and low-tech autonomous systems, groups of transitioners can then 'disconnect' more tranquilly from the great system that risks taking them down with it: they don't have to go to the supermarket, buy one car per family or buy clothes made in China. They are small but practical victories that represent great symbolic victories.

Some 'collapsniks' go even further by proposing an immense generalized disconnection, a kind of giant boycott that would cause the rapid collapse of the global economic system: a 'crash on demand'.[64] In a text published in December 2013, the co-creator of the concept of permaculture, David Holmgren, more pessimistic than ever, expressed his worries over recent discoveries relating to the consequences of global heating. According to him, the only way to avoid too much damage to the biosphere would now be to trigger a fast and radical collapse in the global economic system. He had mainly been anxious, for more than thirty years in fact, about the imminence of peak oil but he is now complaining that it isn't happening fast enough and therefore suggests that all those aware of the issue should disconnect as fast as possible. In his view, if 10 per cent of the population of the industrialized countries managed to fully engage in local resilience initiatives outside the monetary system, the latter could contract to the point of reaching an irreversible tipping point. A 'systemic boycott' – now that's a veritable political blackout! His proposal generated a great deal of controversy among collapsologists around the world, and the argument continues ...

Mobilize an entire people, as in times of war

The transition movement, powerful though it is, would benefit from being coordinated on a larger scale. The remarkable example of a transition to agroecology, as happened in Cuba in the 1990s, shows the importance of the role of the authorities in the speed and power of a great transition. Indeed, the stakes often go beyond local communities, as is the case for rail transport, river management and trade. In the 'special period', the Cuban government took stock of the magnitude of the catastrophes and passed laws in favour of transition.[65] But in Europe and other great democracies, is this still possible? Our generation, which has witnessed only the power that private economic lobbies have over large European institutions, lacks examples suggesting that the large-scale coordinated changes are possible. Yet this is what happened during the two world wars. Governments managed to mobilize considerable power in their pursuit of a common goal, in this case, the annihilation of an enemy. In the 1940s, and thanks to a tremendous war effort, the United States managed to 'give up for a moment the culture of consumption and waste'.[66] In 1943, the Victory Gardens mobilized more than twenty million Americans and produced 30–40 per cent of the country's vegetables! Recycling, car-pooling and even rationing were then the rule in the United States for a few years. These examples, which merit further analysis, are not meant to glorify war or autocratic regimes (North Korea, for example, which was abandoned to its fate after the collapse of the Soviet bloc, just like Cuba, suffered famine under an authoritarian regime). They simply illustrate the fact that, when we organize ourselves for a common purpose, we can move fast and aim high.

It is indeed war situations (and thus times of shortage) that we need to turn to. Could one imagine any policy more characteristic of a collapse than rationing? As the political scientist Mathilde Szuba shows, the industrialized countries have sometimes transgressed their founding principles (the market and private consumption) to implement a policy of rationing.[67] In Paris in 1915, for example, the shortage of basic commodities had caused such an explosive social situation that the city authorities, in the face of government reluctance, decided to set a price for coal and ration it. Rationing can ultimately be considered a policy of solidarity in a world compressed by limits. While 'abundance makes independence possible, [...] the limitation of resources introduces interdependence'.[68] The fate of all inhabitants is bound by a principle of communicating vessels or a 'zero-sum game' where what one person consumes deprives the other person of this good. In this case, the role of the authorities is to rein back the consumption of the rich and to guarantee a vital minimum for the poorest. There are two powerful ideas associated with rationing: 'that of fair shares, calculated equitably on the basis of the quantity available, and that of the equality of all, which involves a suspension of social privileges.'[69]

Unlike France, where rationing during the Second World War left unpleasant memories, in Great Britain, this policy spread a sense of fairness throughout society, which turned out to be very beneficial for social cohesion, according to the testimonies of people who lived through this period. In a surprising way, 'the surveys carried out by the health services during the years 1940–1950 show that the health and longevity of the British, especially children, improved during the rationing period, in particular because part of the population had access to better food'.[70]

What place for democracy?

However, we must not delude ourselves: the catastrophic consequences of climate change and the shocks to the energy and financial systems will inevitably have effects on political systems. 'Democracy will be the first victim of the negative impact on general living conditions that we are planning. [...] By the time the collapse of the species appears conceivable, things will have become too urgent for our slow and complex processes of deliberation. The panic-stricken West will transgress its values of freedom and justice'.[71]

If confidence erodes, if wages and pensions are no longer paid on time or if food shortages become too severe, nothing can guarantee the maintenance of the existing political regimes. Fascism could very easily take advantage of the spreading social unrest, the growing anger of a humiliated people or an involuntary and generalized 'return to the local' caused by repeated economic malfunctions. So Europe could well see, much sooner than expected, the emergence of divided and probably violent societies, far from the cosmopolitan ideal of a 'free' and 'open' world.

Moreover, capitalism has this incredible capacity to prevail wherever societies have suffered traumatic shocks, such as coups and violent repressions (the Philippines, Chile in 1973, etc.).[72] So nothing guarantees that serious economic 'crises' will spontaneously bring about a tranquil and peaceful transition.

If the political and economic elites of the industrialized countries persist in defending a model that now claims to be democratic (but which has clearly become oligarchic),[73] not only will they trigger catastrophes because of their measures to promote 'growth recovery' (see chapters 2, 3, 5 and 8), but they will foment a sense of anger in the population proportional to the (disappointed) hopes they will have aroused.

Proponents of degrowth and transitioners, meanwhile, are very anxious to preserve the democratic ideal, finding that they have the power to act on the local (and often municipal) scale and develop both participative and collaborative practices of governance. As the political scientist Luc Semal notes, the originality of these movements lies in the fact that 'the catastrophist frame is not viewed as a way of locking-in local political debate, but instead as an opportunity to reopen it by inviting people to debate the practical modalities of a degrowth in local energy, now controlled and equitably distributed.'[74]

So, while some will do everything to maintain the current system, some will work to make it even more democratic, while others will accuse it of being the cause of all their misfortunes. In the theoretical and practical worksite constituted by the 'politics of collapse', the question of democracy is certainly not the least important factor. In this respect, the political experience of direct participatory democracy, self-management, federalism and autonomy as developed by libertarian movements could be of the greatest use for these networks of transition.

However, some theoretical issues have still not been addressed: is a mosaic of small local democracies still a democratic project? Is the catastrophist attitude compatible with democratic processes? More precisely, are we really clear-headed when we act *in times of catastrophe*? It now seems essential to devise a way of thinking up policies that will respond calmly and sensibly to the issues that we have described and thus find a compromise between the democratic reflex and the urgent need to cope with catastrophes.

Conclusion:
Hunger is Only the Beginning

'Global overpopulation, overconsumption by the rich, and bad technological choices'[1] have set our industrial civilization on the road to collapse. Major and irreversible systemic shocks may very well take place tomorrow, and the deadline for a large-scale collapse seems to be much closer than we usually imagine, around 2050 or 2100. Nobody can know the exact timing of the sequences that will (in the eyes of future archaeologists) transform a set of catastrophes into a collapse, but it is plausible that this sequence will be the lot of present generations. This is the *intuitive feeling* that we share with many observers, both scientific experts and activists.

It is embarrassing to say this, as the posture is often ridiculed, but we have become catastrophists. Let's make it clear: this does not mean that we desire catastrophes, that we are going to abandon the struggle to mitigate their effects or that we are falling into an irrevocable pessimism. On the contrary! Even if the future is dark, we have to fight because 'waiting does not mean we should be passive'.[2] To be catastrophist, for us, simply means avoiding a posture of denial and taking note of the catastrophes *that are taking place*. We have to learn to see them, to accept their existence and to say goodbye to all that these events will deprive us of. In our opinion, it's this attitude of courage, of consciousness and calm, with our eyes wide open, that will enable us to pursue realistic future paths. This isn't pessimism!

The certainty is that we will never again be in the 'normal' situation that we experienced over the past few decades.[3] First, the engine of thermo-industrial civilization – the energy–finance dynamo – is on the verge of shutdown. Limits have been reached. The era of abundant and cheap fossil fuels is coming to an end, as evidenced by the rush to find unconventional fossil fuels with prohibitively high costs for the environment, the energy supply and the economy. This definitely buries any possibility of getting back to economic growth, and it thus signs the death warrant of a system based on debts – debts that will simply never be repaid.

Second, the exponential material expansion of our civilization has irremediably disrupted the complex natural systems on which it rested. Boundaries have been crossed. Global heating and collapses of biodiversity alone harbinger breakdowns in the food supplies and social, commercial and health systems, i.e., in concrete terms, massive displacements of populations, armed conflicts, epidemics and famines. In this now 'non-linear' world, unforeseen events of greater intensity will be the standard, and it is to be expected that, very often, the solutions we try to apply will disrupt these systems even more.

And third, the ever more complex systems which provide food, water and energy, and which enable politics, finance and the virtual sphere to function, require increasing energy inputs. These infrastructures have become so interdependent, vulnerable and often obsolete that minor interruptions to their flow or supply may endanger the stability of the overall system by causing disproportionate domino effects.

These three states (approaching the limits, exceeding boundaries and increasing complexity) are irreversible and, when combined, they can lead to only one outcome. There were in the past many collapses of civilizations which remained confined to certain regions. Today, globalization has created *global systemic risks*, and this is the first time that a very large-scale, almost global collapse has become possible to envisage. But that won't happen in a single day. A collapse will take different speeds and shapes in different regions and cultures, depending on the vagaries of the environment. So it must be seen as a complex mosaic where nothing can be decided in advance.

To think that every problem will be solved by the return of economic growth is a serious strategic mistake. It erroneously presupposes that a return to growth is possible[4]; and, above all, as long as leaders focus on this goal, no serious policy for preserving the stability of the climate and ecosystems can be implemented to do what is necessary: to significantly and quickly reduce the consumption of fossil fuels. All current debates on the choice between stimulus and austerity are therefore mere distractions from the real issues. In fact, there are not even any 'solutions' to our predicament, just paths we can pursue to adapt to our new reality.

To realize all of this is to trigger a major shift. It is to see that utopia has suddenly changed camp: today, the utopian is whoever believes that everything can just keep going as before. Realism, on the contrary, consists in putting all our remaining energy into a rapid and radical transition, in building local resilience, whether in territorial or human terms.

Towards a general and applied collapsology

'It's precisely because catastrophe is a hateful destiny which we must reject that we need to keep our eyes fixed on it, without ever losing sight of it.'[5] This will be the leitmotif of collapsology. But whereas, for Hans Jonas, 'we prophesy a misfortune so as to stop it happening',[6] we take a further step when we note (thirty-five years later) that it will be very difficult to avoid it and that we can only attempt to mitigate certain of its effects.

We might be criticized for blackening the picture. But those who accuse us of pessimism will have to prove exactly where we are wrong. The burden of proof now lies with the cornucopians. The idea of collapse has become very difficult to evade and, as Clive Hamilton says, the 'pious wish' is not enough.[7]

This book is just a beginning. The logical way forward, in addition to consolidating and updating this data, will involve exploring in greater depth the lines of thought that we opened up in the last two chapters. This will be the true purpose of collapsology, which we define as *the transdisciplinary study of the collapse of our industrial civilization, and what might succeed it, based on the two cognitive modes of reason and intuition and on recognized scientific studies.*

However, it will be of little help in the process of inner transition that everyone is now called upon to undertake. Knowing and understanding is only 10 per cent of the challenge ahead. In parallel, we have to believe, to act accordingly and above all to manage our emotions. All this will involve participating in initiatives that are already situated in *the world after the catastrophe* (the transition movement, Alternatiba, special economic zones, ecovillages, workshops in the Travail qui Relie movement, etc.) and especially through other less austere forms of communication: documentaries, workshops, novels, comics, movies, series, music, dance, theatre, and so on.

The 'hangover' generation

In the 1970s, it was still possible that our society might create 'sustainable development'. It chose not to. Since the 1990s, indeed, everything has continued to accelerate, despite the many warnings. And now it's too late.

It is therefore legitimate to wonder if our ancestors really wanted a 'sustainable' society. The answer is no. In any case, some ancestors, those who at a given time had the power to impose technological and political decisions on others, chose – *quite knowingly* – an unsustainable society. For example, the question of the exhaustion (and therefore wastage) of fossil fuels arose as soon as they started to be extracted around 1800.[8] Some people argued that they should be used sensibly, but their voices were marginalized.[9] In 1866, the British economist William Stanley Jevons aptly summed up this question of coal (which can be extended to include all fossil fuels) to 'a historic choice between a brief grandeur and a longer mediocrity'.[10] You will easily guess which option he preferred and which one actually won …

The work of historians is essential today if we are to understand what the brilliant economist Nicholas Georgescu-Roegen lucidly sensed in the 1970s: 'It's as if the human race had chosen to lead a brief but exciting life, leaving to less ambitious species a long but monotonous existence.'[11] But will all of us, the descendants of these ambitious ancestors who are coming to the end of this 'brief greatness', and suffering its consequences, even have the choice of *at least* returning to a modest period of 'long mediocrity'? We can't even be sure of that any more.

After all, there are many of us on Earth, with an aggressive and unpredictable climate, destroyed and polluted eco-systems (who will then be able to detect pollution?) and a biological and cultural diversity that is rapidly diminishing. If we don't collectively all wake up in time, then, in the great silence of the post-industrial world, we may return to a far more precarious situation than that in the Middle Ages. In this case, it would paradoxically be the proponents of unbridled growth who will have forced us all back to the Stone Age.

These celebrants of 'progress' venerated the brief grandeur, the party time we have been celebrating for two centuries, without thought for the morrow, where everyone was out to jump about, to move and shout louder, to forget all the rest, to forget themselves. They always needed more energy, more objects, speed, control. They needed to have more of everything. Now, for them, it's hangover time: 'the party's over!'[12] Ultimately, modernity will not have died of its postmodern philosophical wounds but because it has run out of energy. And if amphetamines and antidepressants were the pills of the productivist world, resilience, sobriety and low tech will be the aspirins of the hangover generation.

Other ways of partying

These 'progressives' also mocked 'long mediocrity'. But was it all that mediocre? Today, the paths we might pursue – and there *are* paths – are barely marked, and they lead to a radical change in life, a life less complex, smaller, more modest and respectful of the limits and boundaries of the living world. Collapse is not the end but the beginning of our future. We will reinvent ways of partying, ways of being present to the world and to oneself, to others and to the beings around us.

The end of the world? It would be too easy; the planet is there, rustling with life; there are responsibilities to take and a future to trace. It's time to behave like adults.

In our meetings with the public, we have been surprised to find much joy and laughter that did not try to conceal a certain despair but was expressed with some relief. Some even thanked us for giving words and emotions to a profound discomfort that they could not themselves voice. Others confided in us that they had even given their lives new meaning! We were not alone anymore. Indeed, there are far more of us. In difficult times, networks are formed. And we're growing up.

For the Children

The rising hills, the slopes,
of statistics
lie before us.
The steep climb
of everything, going up,
up, as we all
go down.

In the next century
or the one beyond that,
they say,
are valleys, pastures,
we can meet there in peace
if we make it.

To climb these coming crests
one word to you, to
you and your children:

stay together
learn the flowers
go light

Gary Snyder, *Turtle Island*, 1974[1]

Postscript by Yves Cochet

Is there any subject more important than that which is treated in this book? No. Is there any subject more neglected than this one? No. This is the political paradox of our world: we continue to go about our business with, of course, the firm intention of improving our lot by carrying out a few reforms, but there is never any question about our disappearance in the short term as a civilization, whereas – as this book amply demonstrates – we have never had so many indications of the possibility of an imminent global collapse. This is not surprising on the part of politicians, here and elsewhere, today and in the past. What regime, what leader would produce a catastrophist analysis of the state of the world and draw the conclusion that the direction and public policies of the society he governs need to be radically changed? This phenomenon of denial of reality is not simply due to the contradiction between the short term of politics ('I must remember I'm up for re-election soon') and the long duration of ecology (repairing the ecosphere needs a long time);

no, this phenomenon stems first and foremost from the limitations of the human cognitive apparatus and the constraints of social psychology.

In short, faced with the evocation of an extraordinary and monstrous event still to come – here 'the collapse of the world' – no human being can imagine its effects, even though this event is the consequence of human actions. This discrepancy is one of the characteristics of the thermo-industrial modernity analysed by the philosopher Günther Anders, who called these events 'supraliminal'. We are unable to form a complete mental image of it or to anticipate all its repercussions. This is true of the authors of this book and of myself. However much we examine the innumerable data and draw on them for our argument, it is impossible for us, even from a systemic point of view, to forge a complete rational representation of what 'the collapse of the world' might be. Simply, we feel an intuition of it, almost a certainty. It is even more impossible, if I can put it this way, to represent the consequences of such an event. How many people will die as a result of this collapse?

This intuitive certainty of collapse, felt by a few people, becomes doubly confused when it clashes with the reactions of others. Indeed, there then comes into play a specular mechanism that explains, better than any accumulation of individual wills, society's inaction when a supraliminal event looms. Suppose I am convinced of the impending collapse and that I try to share this belief with my friends and relatives or with random people. It is possible that a few will agree with me but most of the time, at least for now, the majority, even people quite well informed about global ecological issues, will take refuge first in denial, in cognitive dissonance. No collective action will result, no attempt to arrest this collapse. And, paradoxically, even if a majority of people (in France, for example) were finally convinced of the impending collapse, it is unlikely that this majority would organize to act effectively against this threat. Effectively, that is to say, by rapidly implementing vast resources to fight against this hypothesis being realized, with all the changes in individual and collective behaviour that this would require. Examples abound of such situations where, in a given territory, a majority of people believe sincerely in a horrendous fact, but where no one (or almost no one) acts against this fact. This is true of the climate change that a majority of European citizens recognizes as of anthropic origin, but where individual behaviour and public policies to tackle this phenomenon have been deplorably weak for the past twenty-five years. This was true of the dictatorship of Saddam Hussein during the last quarter of the twentieth century – this dictatorship was considered cruel by the majority of Iraqis, but the accumulation of these individual opinions did not lead to the overthrow of the regime. Why did Iraqis tolerate this tyranny they hated? How are we to explain this type of apparent contradiction? The present book has shown you conclusively that the world is on the verge of collapse; like you, a majority of readers may be stunned by this demonstration and persuaded of the imminence of the end of the world as we know it; and ... they will do nothing. No (or almost no) personal or political action of the necessary scope will ensue.

We will try to explain this social quirk by a cognitivist approach, as we did earlier, by evoking the limits of individual psychology. This time, it is the philosopher Jean-Louis Vullierme to whom we owe the foundations of this point of view of social psychology. What triggers the action of an individual is not his/her opinion or will but the question as to whether s/he would act only on condition that a sufficiently large number of other people also act. Collective (political) action is not an accumulative phenomenon of individual

wills to act but the emerging result of representations that
everyone creates by observing the representations of others.
Society is a system of cross-representations between individuals: I represent to myself the way others represent things,
and me, to themselves. In other words, the models of the
world possessed by individuals, especially their models of
themselves, are based on the models of the world owned
by others, especially the models that others have of these
individuals (Vullierme calls this cognitive interaction 'spec-
ularity'). What determines an individual's behaviour is
therefore the system of models that this individual possesses.
According to this hypothesis, will is thus not a primary reality
but a reality derived from specular interaction. The individual who is cognisant of the collapse does not wonder if s/he
wants to change his/her life but only if s/he would do so if a
number of others also did so. With each person being placed
in the same situation as others, the collapse will be reduced,
not thanks to the will of all but thanks to their combined
representations – according to the way each person gauges
the actual capacity of those who surround him/her to change
their lives. What about the denial of collapse by decision
makers? The specular dynamic still functions inexorably.
The propagation of beliefs in the impending collapse can
only be slow within a political world obsessed with rivalry.
So much so that even though all the world's leaders, as under
the impact of some revelation, were suddenly convinced
that a collapse was imminent, they would start by asking
if their political friends and rivals shared this belief or not.
Everyone would know that the catastrophe was imminent
but would not know that the others knew. Everyone would
watch out for the others to make a faux pas – the public dis-
closure of the force of their belief – so ultimately nobody
would disclose this belief. This belief, known to everyone,
would not be common knowledge. And even less would it be

a common action since it would then be necessary to upset public policies by radically altering the production and consumption patterns of industrialized societies. This would imply that the citizens themselves possess this model of the world – this belief in an imminent collapse – and accept its consequences in terms of drastically changing their mode of life. The denial of the collapse, then, is not due to people as individuals being unreasonable or insufficiently informed; it is a systemic effect that emerges from specular relationships. So, if many communities of transitioners and anti-growth protestors fail to emerge, collapse is inevitable, not because the scientific knowledge of its coming is too uncertain but because the social psychology embedded in human beings will not allow them to take the right decisions at the right time.

However, like the authors of this book, I believe that no one can become a collapsologist without feeling a chronic tremor on obtaining the results of his/her research. More than in other areas, reflection and emotion are intimately mixed in an ecological eschatology where issues of life and death, personal and collective, are the very objects of the investigation. We cannot approach this investigation ingenuously, believing that our lives will not be turned upside down as a result. We cannot speak publicly about global collapse without being certain that what we are saying will resound intensely in each of our listeners. Collapsology is a school of responsibility. It then leads directly to an ethics based on a power that transcends us individually, as does the collapse we are exploring. This metaphysical instance is compassion, or empathy, or altruism, as you wish. But we do not feel this moral force as external to ourselves, dictated by some dogma or religion: it belongs to our being since both the images and the thoughts of collapse that now populate our minds are mixed, as in an indecomposable alloy that cannot be reduced to it various components. Note that I am not saying that the study of collapse leads to humanitarian wisdom and to the love of one's neighbour. Paradoxically, it can even sometimes be accompanied by misanthropic ruminations against those blind human beings, my sisters and my brothers, who ignore the threats to the world and continue innocently to lead their little lives. I am simply stating that collapsology, by its very object, leads to the distinction between good and evil, with good being any action that will reduce the number of deaths, and evil being indifference to this criterion or, worse, morbid pleasure at a larger number of deaths. In this sense, I can pass a judgment of moral responsibility on myself and on others.

Yves Cochet, former Minister of the Environment, President of the Institut Momentum

Notes

For further information go to: www.collapsologie.fr. Some parts of our text have already been published in the following articles:

Pablo Servigne and Raphaël Stevens, 'Résilience en temps de catastrophe', *Barricade*, 2013 (ch. 10 of the present book on mutual aid).

Pablo Servigne and Raphaël Stevens, 'L'anthropocène. L'ère de l'incertitude', *Barricade*, 2013 (ch. 1).

Pablo Servigne and Raphaël Stevens, 'Alors, ça vient? Pourquoi la transition se fait attendre', *Barricade*, 2014 (ch. 4).

Pablo Servigne and Raphaël Stevens, 'Les inégalités, un facteur d'effondrement', *Etopia*, 2014 (ch. 8, section 'An original model: HANDY').

Pablo Servigne, 'L'effet domino chez les animaux', *Imagine demain le monde* 106, 2014: 46–7 (ch. 3, section 'Who will kill the last animal on the planet?').

Pablo Servigne, 'Lorsque tout bascule', *Imagine demain le monde* 107, 2015: 40–1 (ch. 3, section 'What happens when we cross different Rubicons?').

Introduction: We'll Definitely Need to Tackle the Subject One of These Days . . .

1 Yves Cochet, 'L'effondrement, catabolique ou catastrophique?', *Institut Momentum*, 27 May 2011.

2 Paul R. Ehrlich and Anne H. Ehrlich, 'Can a collapse of global civilization be avoided?', *Philosophical Transactions of the Royal Society B* 280(1754), 2013: 20122845.

3 Jonathan Brown, 'Mankind must go green or die, says Prince Charles', *The Independent*, 23 November 2012.

4 Christophe Bonneuil and Jean-Baptiste Fressoz, *L'Événement Anthropocène. La Terre, l'histoire et nous* (Paris: Seuil, 2013).

5 For example, Jean-Pierre Dupuy, *Pour un catastrophisme éclairé: quand l'impossible est certain* (Paris: Seuil, 2002); Hicham-Stéphane Hafeissa, *La Fin du monde et de l'humanité. Essai de généalogie du discours écologique* (Paris: PUF, 2014); Patrick Viveret, *Du bon usage de la fin d'un monde* (Paris: Les Liens qui Libèrent, 2012); Michaël Foessel, *Après la fin du monde. Critique de la raison apocalyptique* (Paris: Seuil, 2012).

6 Jared Diamond, *Collapse: How Societies Choose to Fail or Survive* (London: Penguin, 2006).

7 Rob Hopkins, *The Transition Handbook: From Oil Dependency to Local Resilience* (Totnes: Green, 2008), and *The Power of Just Doing Stuff: How Local Action Can Change the World* (Totnes: Green, 2013).

8 http://www.institutmomentum.org.

Chapter 1 The Accelerating Vehicle

1 Will Steffen et al., 'The trajectory of the Anthropocene: The great acceleration', *The Anthropocene Review* 2: 81–98.

2 Albert Jacquard is a geneticist, essayist and humanist. See Albert Jacquard, *L'Équation du nénuphar: les plaisirs de la science* (Paris: Calmann-Lévy, 1998).

3 The interested reader can find a series of highly instructive examples of the way an exponential behaves in ch. 2 of Donella Meadows et al., *The Limits to Growth* (New York: Universe Books, 1972).

4 C. Hui, 'Carrying capacity, population equilibrium, and

environment's maximal load', *Ecological Modelling* 192, 2006: 317–20.

5 Mathis Wackernagel and William E. Rees, 'Perceptual and structural barriers to investing in natural capital: Economics from an ecological footprint perspective', *Ecological Economics* 20(1), 1997: 3–24.

6 Donella Meadows et al., *Limits to Growth: The 30-Year Update* (White River Junction, VT: Chelsea Green Publishing, 2004).

7 As presented by Will Steffen et al., 'The Anthropocene: Are humans now overwhelming the great forces of nature?', *AMBIO: A Journal of the Human Environment* 36(8), 2007: 614–21.

8 Henri Bergson, *Creative Evolution*, trans. Arthur Mitchell (London: Macmillan & Co., 1922), pp. 145–6.

9 Fridolin Krausmann et al., 'Growth in global materials use, GDP and population during the 20th century', *Ecological Economics* 68(10), 2009: 2696–705.

10 Hartmut Rosa, *Social Acceleration: A New Theory of Modernity*, trans. Jonathan Trejo-Mathys (New York: Columbia University Press, 2013).

11 Hartmut Rosa, 'Accélération et dépression. Réflexions sur le rapport au temps de notre époque', *Rhizome* 43, 2012: 4–13.

12 Rosa, 'Accélération et dépression'.

13 This is the question which the think tank known as the Club of Rome asked the team comprised of Donella Meadows, Dennis Meadows, Jørgen Randers and William W. Behrens III to consider. Their report was published in 1972 as 'Limits to growth'. See also Serge Latouche, *L'Âge des limites* (Paris: Mille et une nuits, 2013).

Chapter 2 When the Engine Dies (Limits that Cannot be Crossed)

1 International Energy Agency, *World Energy Outlook 2010*.

2 Richard Miller and Steve Sorrell, 'The future of oil supply', *Philosophical Transactions of the Royal Society A* 372(2006): 2014.

3 'BP Statistical Review of World Energy 2014'. http://large.stan ford.edu/courses/2014/ph240/milic1/docs/bpreview.pdf.

4 Steve Andrews and Randy Udall, 'The oil production story: Pre- and post-peak nations', *Association for the Study of Peak Oil & Gas USA*, 2014.

5 Steve Sorrell et al., 'Shaping the global oil peak: A review of the evidence on field sizes, reserve growth, decline rates and depletion rates', *Energy* 37(1), 2012: 709–24.

6 Richard Miller and Steve Sorrell, 'Preface of the special issue on the future of oil supply', *Philosophical Transactions of the Royal Society A* 372(2006), 2014: 20130301.

7 Steve Sorrell et al., 'An assessment of the evidence for a near-term peak in global oil production', UK Energy Research Centre, 2009.

8 United States Joint Forces Command, 'The Joint Operating Environment 2010'. https://fas.org/man/eprint/joe2010.pdf

9 Bundeswehr, 'Peak Oil: Sicherheitspolitische Implikationen knapper Ressourcen', Planungsamt der Bundeswehr, 2010.

10 J. Murray and D. King, 'Climate policy: Oil's tipping point has passed', *Nature* 481(7382), 2012: 433–5.

11 ITPOES, 'The oil crunch: A wake-up call for the UK economy', Second Report of the UK Industry Taskforce on Peak Oil and Energy Security, 2010.

12 J. R. Hallock et al., 'Forecasting the limits to the availability and diversity of global conventional oil supply: Validation', *Energy* 64, 2014: 130–53.

13 Madelon L. Finkel and Jake Hays, 'The implications of unconventional drilling for natural gas: A global public health concern', *Public Health* 127(10), 2013: 889–93; H. Else, 'Fracking splits opinion', *Professional Engineering* 25(2), 2012: 26.

14 William Ellsworth, 'Injection-induced earthquakes', *Science* 341(614), 2013: 1225942.

15 R. J. Davies et al., 'Oil and gas wells and their integrity: Implications for shale and unconventional resource exploitation', *Marine and Petroleum Geology* 56, 2014: 239–54.

16 J. Henry Fair, 'Radionuclides in fracking wastewater', *Environmental Health Perspectives* 122(2), 2014: A50–5.

17 Cutler J. Cleveland and Peter A. O'Connor, 'Energy return on investment (EROI) of oil shale', *Sustainability* 3(11), 2011: 2307–22.

18 Bridget R. Scanlon et al., 'Comparison of water use for hydraulic fracturing for shale oil and gas production versus conventional oil', *Environmental Science & Technology* 48(20), 2014: 12386–93.

19 Erik Stokstad, 'Will fracking put too much fizz in your water?', *Science*, 344(6191), 2014: 1468–71.

20 US Energy Information Administration, 'As cash flow flattens, major energy companies increase debt, sell assets', *Today in Energy*, 29 July 2014, http://www.eia.gov/todayinenergy/detail.cfm?id=17311.

21 Asjylyn Loder, 'Shakeout threatens shale patch as frackers go for broke', Bloomberg, 27 May 2014, http://www.bloomberg.com/news/2014-05-26/shakeout-threatens-shale-patch-as-frackers-go-for-broke.html.

22 Sorrell et al., 'An assessment of the evidence for a near-term peak'.

23 J. David Hughes, 'Energy: A reality check on the shale revolution', *Nature* 494(7437), 2013: 307–8.

24 For example, Daniel Yergin, 'US energy is changing the world again', *Financial Times*, 16 November 2012; L. Maugeri, 'The shale oil boom: A US phenomenon', Belfer Center for Science and International Affairs, Harvard Kennedy School, 2013, Discussion Paper tbc2013-05.

25 B. K. Sovacool, 'Cornucopia or curse? Reviewing the costs and benefits of shale gas hydraulic fracturing (fracking)', *Renewable and Sustainable Energy Reviews* 37, 2014: 249–64.

26 US Energy Information Administration, 'Annual Energy Outlook 2014', p. 17.

27 Quoted in Sorrell et al., 'An assessment of the evidence for a near-term peak'.

28 Charles Emmerson and Glada Lahn, 'Arctic opening: Opportunity and risk in the High North', Chatham House-Lloyd's, 2013.

29 James Marriott, 'Oil projects too far – banks and investors refuse finance for Arctic oil', *Platform Education Research London*, 24 April 2012.

30 Audrey Garric, 'Après une série noire, Shell renonce à forer en Arctique cette année', *Le Monde*, 28 February 2013.

31 Guy Chazan, 'Total warns against oil drilling in Arctic', *Financial Times*, 25 September 2012.

32 G. R. Timilsina, 'Biofuels in the long-run global energy supply mix for transportation', *Philosophical Transactions of the Royal Society A* 372(2006), 2014.

33 Tatsuji Koizumi, 'Biofuels and food security in the US, the EU and other countries', in *Biofuels and Food Security* (New York: Springer International Publishing, 2014), pp. 59–78.

34 G. Maggio and G. Cacciola, 'When will oil, natural gas, and coal peak?', *Fuel* 98, 2012: 111–23; Philip Shearman et al., 'Are we approaching "peak timber" in the tropics?', *Biological Conservation* 151(1), 2012: 17–21; Russell D. Warman, 'Global wood production from natural forests has peaked', *Biodiversity and Conservation* 23(5), 2014: 1063–78; Michael Dittmar, 'The end of cheap uranium', *Science of the Total Environment* 461–2, 2013: 792–8.

35 Ugo Bardi et al., *Extracted: How the Quest for Mineral Wealth Is Plundering the Planet* (White River Junction VT: Chelsea Green Publishing, 2014).

36 Chris Clugston, 'Increasing global nonrenewable natural resource scarcity: An analysis', *Energy Bulletin* 4(6), 2010.

37 Dana Cordell et al., 'The story of phosphorus: Global food security and food for thought', *Global Environmental Change* 19(2), 2009: 292–305.

38 Ransom A. Myers and Boris Worm, 'Rapid worldwide depletion of predatory fish communities', *Nature* 423(6937), 2003: 280–3.

39 Peter H. Gleick and Meena Palaniappan, 'Peak water limits to freshwater withdrawal and use', *PNAS* 107(25), 2010: 11155–62.

40 Philippe Bihouix, *L'Âge des low tech. Vers une civilisation techniquement soutenable* (Paris: Seuil, 2014), pp. 66–7.

41 Richard Heinberg, *Peak Everything: Waking Up to the Century of Decline in Earth's Resources* (West Hoathly: Clairview Books, 2007).

42 Barclays Research Data, quoted in Steven Kopits, 'Oil and economic growth: a supply-constrained view', Columbia University, Center on Global Energy Policy, 11 February 2014, http://tiny url.com/mhkju2k.

43 Cutler J. Cleveland, 'Net energy from the extraction of oil and gas in the United States', *Energy* 30, 2005: 769–82.

44 N. Gagnon et al., 'A preliminary investigation of energy return on energy investment for global oil and gas production', *Energies* 2(3), 2009: 490–503.

45 David J. Murphy and Charles A. S. Hall, 'Year in review – EROI or energy return on (energy) invested', *Annals of the New York Academy of Sciences* 1185(1), 2010: 102–18.

46 Charles A. S. Hall et al., 'EROI of different fuels and the implications for society', *Energy Policy* 64, 2014: 141–52.

47 Pedro A. Prieto and Charles A. S. Hall, *Spain's Photovoltaic
Revolution: The Energy Return on Investment* (New York: Springer,
2013).

48 Hall et al., 'EROI of different fuels'.

49 D. Weißbach et al., 'Energy intensities, EROIs (energy returned
on invested), and energy payback times of electricity generating
power plants', *Energy* 52, 2013: 210–21.

50 Brad Plumer, 'We're damming up every last big river on Earth.
Is that really a good idea?', Vox, 28 October 2014, http://www.
vox.com/2014/10/28/7083487/the-world-is-building-thousands-
of-new-dams-is-that-really-a-good-idea.

51 Christiane Zarfl et al., 'A global boom in hydropower dam construction', *Aquatic Sciences*, 2014: 1–10.

52 Gail E. Tverberg, 'Converging energy crises – and how our
current situation differs from the past', *Our Finite World*, 29
May 2014, http://ourfiniteworld.com/2014/05/29/converging-
energy-crises-and-how-our-current-situation-differs-from-the-
past/.

53 Charles A. S. Hall et al., 'What is the minimum EROI that a
sustainable society must have?', *Energies* 2, 2009: 25-47.

54 Jessica G. Lambert et al., 'Energy, EROI and quality of life',
Energy Policy 64, 2014: 153–67.

55 Benoît Thévard, 'La diminution de l'énergie nette, frontière
ultime de l'Anthropocène', *Institut Momentum*, 2013.

56 Carey W. King and Charles A. S. Hall, 'Relating financial and
energy return on investment', *Sustainability* 3(10), 2011: 1810–
32; Matthew K. Heun and Martin De Wit, 'Energy return on
(energy) invested (EROI), oil prices, and energy transitions',
Energy Policy 40, 2012: 147–58.

57 Bardi et al., *Extracted*.

58 See Gaël Giraud et al., *Produire plus, polluer moins: l'impossible
découplage?* (Paris: Les Petits Matins, 2014).

59 David J. Murphy, 'The implications of the declining energy
return on investment of oil production', *Philosophical Transactions
of the Royal Society A* 372(2006), 2013: 20130126.

60 James D. Hamilton, 'Causes and consequences of the oil shock
of 2007–08', *National Bureau of Economic Research*, 2009; Charles

Hall and Kent Klitgaard, *Energy and the Wealth of Nations: Understanding the Biophysical Economy* (New York: Springer, 2012).

61 Gail E. Tverberg, 'Low oil prices: Sign of a debt bubble collapse, leading to the end of oil supply?', *Our Finite World*, 21 September 2014, http://ourfiniteworld.com/2014/09/21/low-oil-prices-sign-of-a-debt-bubble-collapse-leading-to-the-end-of-oil-supply.

62 Gail E. Tverberg, 'Oil supply limits and the continuing financial crisis', *Energy* 37(1), 2012: 27–34.

63 E. Ailworth, 'Drillers cut expansion plans as oil prices drop', *Wall Street Journal*, 6 November 2014.

64 International Energy Agency, *World Energy Outlook 2014*.

65 Matthieu Auzanneau, 'Pétrole: le calme avant la tempête, d'après l'Agence internationale de l'énergie', *Oil Man*, 19 November 2014, http://petrole.blog.lemonde.fr/2014/11/19/petrole-le-calme-avant-la-tempete-dapres-lagence-internationale-de-lenergie/.

66 Robert M. May et al., 'Complex systems: Ecology for bankers', *Nature* 451(7181), 2008: 893–5.

67 Gail E. Tverberg, 'World oil production at 3/31/2014 – Where are we headed?', *Our Finite World*, 23 June 2014, http://ourfiniteworld.com/2014/07/23/world-oil-production-at-3312014-where-are-we-headed/.

68 Marco Lagi et al., *The Food Crises and Political Instability in North Africa and the Middle East*, New England Complex Systems Institute, 2011.

69 Jeremy Leggett, *The Energy of Nations: Risk Blindness and the Road to Renaissance* (London: Routledge, 2013), p. xiii.

Chapter 3 Leaving the Road (Boundaries that Can be Crossed)

1 According to the IPCC report published on 27 September 2013 (a very high certainty of 95 per cent). See also John Cook et al., 'Quantifying the consensus on anthropogenic global warming in the scientific literature', *Environmental Research Letters* 8(2), 2013: 024024.

2 Hans Joachim Schellnhuber et al., 'Turn down the heat: Why a 4°C warmer world must be avoided', Washington, DC, World Bank, 2012.

3 Stefan Rahmstorf et al., 'Comparing climate projections to observations up to 2011', *Environmental Research Letters* 7(4), 2012: 044035.

4 Dim Coumou and Stefan Rahmstorf, 'A decade of weather extremes', *Nature Climate Change* 2, 2012: 491–6.

5 Jean-Marie Robine et al., 'Death toll exceeded 70,000 in Europe during the summer of 2003', *Comptes rendus biologies* 331(2), 2008: 171–8.

6 There is even one study showing that, in some currently populated regions, human beings would not be able to survive after 2100. See S. C. Sherwood and M. Hubert, 'An adaptability limit to climate change due to heat stress', *PNAS* 107(21), 2010: 9552–5.

7 David Barriopedro et al., 'The hot summer of 2010: redrawing the temperature record map of Europe', *Science* 332(6026), 2005: 220–4.

8 Kirstin Dow and Thomas. E. Downing, *The Atlas of Climate Change* (Berkeley, CA: University of California Press, 2007).

9 J. D. Steinbruner et al. (ed.), *Climate and Social Stress: Implications for Security Analysis* (Washington, DC: National Academies Press, 2012).

10 WHO, 'Climate change and health', World Health Organization Fact Sheet 266, 2013.

11 Werner A. Kurz et al., 'Mountain pine beetle and forest carbon feedback to climate change', *Nature* 452(7190), 2008: 987–90.

12 See Brendan Choat et al., 'Global convergence in the vulnerability of forests to drought', *Nature* 491(7426), 2012: 752–6.

13 Andrew Shepherd et al., 'A reconciled estimate of ice-sheet mass balance', *Science* 338(6111), 2012: 1183–9.

14 Gwynne Dyer, *Climate Wars. The Fight for Survival as the World Overheats* (Oxford: Oneworld, 2010), pp. 55–6.

15 Hans Joachim Schellnhuber et al., 'Turn down the heat: Why a 4°C warmer world must be avoided', Washington, DC, World Bank, 2012.

16 D. D. Zhang et al., 'The causality analysis of climate change and large-scale human crisis', PNAS 108(42), 2011: 17296–301; D. D. Zhang et al., 'Global climate change, war, and population decline in recent human history', *PNAS* 104(49), 2007: 19214–19.

17 Jacob Schewe et al., 'Multimodel assessment of water scarcity under climate change', *PNAS* 111(9), 2014: 3245–50.

18 David B. Lobell et al., 'Climate trends and global crop production since 1980', *Science* 333(6042), 2011: 616–20.

19 K. Kristensen et al., 'Winter wheat yield response to climate variability in Denmark', *The Journal of Agricultural Science* 149(1), 2011: 33–47; J. E. Olesen et al., 'Impacts and adaptation of European crop production systems to climate change', *European Journal of Agronomy* 34(2), 2011: 96–112.

20 J. H. Christensen et al., 'Regional climate projections', in S. Solomon, D. Qin, M. Manning et al. (eds), *Climate Change 2007: The Physical Science Basis* (Cambridge: Cambridge University Press, 2007), p. 996; A. Dai, 'Increasing drought under global warming in observations and models', *Nature Climate Change* 3(1), 2012: 52–8.

21 Z. W. Kundzewicz, 'Assessing river flood risk and adaptation in Europe – review of projections for the future', *Mitigation and Adaptation Strategies for Global Change* 15(7), 2010: 641–56.

22 M. Bindi and J. E. Olesen, 'The responses of agriculture in Europe to climate change', *Regional Environmental Change* 11(1), 2011: 151–8; M. T. Harrison, 'Characterizing drought stress and trait influence on maize yield under current and future conditions', *Global Change Biology* 20(3), 2014: 867–78.

23 Dyer, *Climate Wars*, p. 58.

24 Dyer, *Climate Wars*, p. 56.

25 F. Gemenne, 'Climate-induced population displacements in a 4°C+ world', *Philosophical Transactions of the Royal Society A* 369(1934), 2011: 182–95.

26 M. T. van Vliet et al., 'Vulnerability of US and European electricity supply to climate change', *Nature Climate Change* 2(9), 2012: 676–81.

27 K. M. Campbell et al., 'The age of consequences: the foreign policy and national security implications of global climate change', Washington, DC, Center for Strategic and International Studies, 2007, https://csis-prod.s3.amazonaws.com/s3fs-public/legacy_files/files/media/csis/pubs/071105_ageofconsequences.pdf, p. 77.

28 Dyer, *Climate Wars*, p. 23.

29 Dyer, *Climate Wars*, p. 60.

30 J. Kiehl, 'Lessons from Earth's Past', *Science* 331(6014), 2011: 158–9.

31 James Lovelock, *The Revenge of Gaia: Why the Earth is Fighting Back – and How We Can Still Save Humanity* (London: Penguin, 2007). Quoted in Dyer, *Climate Wars*, p. 26.

32 J. Hansen et al., 'Climate sensitivity, sea level and atmospheric carbon dioxide', *Philosophical Transactions of the Royal Society A* 371, 2013: 20120294.

33 S. L. Pimm et. al., 'The biodiversity of species and their rates of extinction, distribution, and protection', *Science* 344(6187), 2014: 1246752.

34 Richard McLellan et al. (eds), *Living Planet Report 2014: Species and Spaces, People and Places* (Gland, Switzerland: World Wildlife Fund, 2014).

35 Robert M. May, 'Ecological science and tomorrow's world', *Philosophical Transactions of the Royal Society B* 365(1537), 2010: 41–7; W. F. Laurance et al., 'Averting biodiversity collapse in tropical forest protected areas', *Nature* 489(7415), 2012: 290–4.

36 Pimm et al., 'The biodiversity of species'.

37 D. Sanders et al., 'The loss of indirect interactions leads to cascading extinctions of carnivores', *Ecology Letters* 16(5), 2013: 664–9.

38 J. J. Lever et al., 'The sudden collapse of pollinator communities', *Ecology Letters* 17(3), 2014: 350–9.

39 S. H. Anderson et al., 'Cascading effects of bird functional extinction reduce pollination and plant density', *Science* 331(6020), 2011: 1068–71.

40 R. R. Dunn et al., 'The sixth mass coextinction: Are most endangered species parasites and mutualists?', *Philosophical Transactions of the Royal Society B* 276(1670), 2009: 3037–45.

41 See Rachel Carson, *Silent Spring* (Boston, MA: Houghton Mifflin, 1962); in this book, Carson predicted the dramatic consequences of pesticides on ecosystems.

42 R. Dirzo et al., 'Defaunation in the Anthropocene', *Science* 345(6195), 2014: 401–6.

43 Richard McLellan et al (eds), *Living Planet Report 2014*, pp. 8–9.

44 W. J. Ripple et al., 'Status and ecological effects of the world's largest carnivores', *Science* 343(6167), 2014: 1241484.

45 J. A. Estes et al., 'Trophic downgrading of planet Earth', *Science* 333(6040), 2011: 301–6.

46 D. J. McCauley et al., 'Marine defaunation: Animal loss in the global ocean', *Science* 347(6219), 2015: 1255641.

47 B. S. Halpern et al., 'A global map of human impact on marine ecosystems', *Science* 319(5865), 2008: 948–52.

48 Ransom A. Myers and Boris Worm, 'Rapid worldwide depletion of predatory fish communities', *Nature* 423(6937), 2003: 280–3.

49 J. B. Jackson, 'Ecological extinction and evolution in the brave new ocean', *PNAS* 105, 2008: 11458–65.

50 K. Swing, 'Conservation: Inertia is speeding fish-stock declines', *Nature* 494(7437), 2013: 314.

51 Anderson et al., 'Cascading effects of bird functional extinction', pp. 1068–71.

52 Stéphane Foucart, 'Le déclin massif des insectes menace l'agriculture', *Le Monde*, 26 June 2014; I. Newton, 'The recent declines of farmland bird populations in Britain: An appraisal of causal factors and conservation actions', *Ibis* 146(4), 2004: 579–600.

53 C. A. Hallmann et al., 'Declines in insectivorous birds are associated with high neonicotinoid concentrations', *Nature* 511(7509), 2014: 341–3; George Monbiot, 'Another silent spring?', *The Guardian*, 16 July 2014.

54 Dirzo et al., 'Defaunation in the Anthropocene'.

55 In France, according to the ecologist François Ramade, the number of beehives fell from 2 million in 1996 to 600,000 today.

56 Foucart, 'Le déclin massif des insectes'.

57 Erik Stokstad, 'The empty forest', *Science* 345(6195), 2014: 396–9.

58 A. D. Barnosky et al., 'Has the Earth's sixth mass extinction already arrived?', *Nature* 471(7336), 2011: 51–7.

59 D. U. Hooper et al., 'A global synthesis reveals biodiversity loss as a major driver of ecosystem change', *Nature* 486(7401), 2012: 105–8; Dirzo et al., 'Defaunation in the Anthropocene'.

60 A. S. MacDougall et al., 'Diversity loss with persistent human disturbance increases vulnerability to ecosystem collapse', *Nature* 494(7435), 2013: 86–9.

61 J. V. Yule et al., 'Biodiversity, extinction, and humanity's future: The ecological and evolutionary consequences of human population and resource use', *Humanities* 2(2), 2013: 147–59.

62 J. M. Morvan et al., 'Écosystèmes forestiers et virus Ebola', Third Colloquium of the network of the Pasteur Institute and associated institutes, 14-15 October 1999; B. A. Wilcox and B. Ellis, 'Les forêts et les maladies infectieuses émergentes chez l'homme', Unasylva (FAO), 2006; J. A. Ginsburg, 'How saving West African forests might have prevented the Ebola epidemic', *The Guardian*, 3 October 2014.

63 Harold Thibault, 'Dans le Sichuan, des "hommes-abeilles" pollinisent à la main les vergers', *Le Monde*, 23 April 2014.

64 R. Costanza, 'The value of the world's ecosystem services and natural capital', *Ecological Economics* 25(1), 1998: 3–15.

65 C. B. Field et al., 'Climate Change 2014: Impacts, adaptation, and vulnerability', Contribution of Working Group II to the Fifth Assessment Report of the IPCC, 2014.

66 Eugenia V. Bragina et al., 'Rapid declines of large mammal populations after the collapse of the Soviet Union', *Conservation Biology* 29(3), June 2015: 844–53.

67 F. Krausmann et al., 'Global human appropriation of net primary production doubled in the 20th century', *PNAS* 110(25), 2013: 10324–9.

68 Christophe Bonneuil and Jean-Baptiste Fressoz, *L'Événement Anthropocène. La Terre, l'histoire et nous* (Paris: Seuil, 2013), p. 225, note.

69 Bonneuil and Fressoz, *L'Événement Anthropocène*, p. 226, note.

70 A. E. Cahill et al., 'How does climate change cause extinction?', *Proceedings of the Royal Society B* 280(1750), 2013: 20121890; C. Bellard et al., 'Impacts of climate change on the future of biodiversity', *Ecology Letters* 15(4), 2012: 365–77; Field et al., 'Climate Change 2014'.

71 Yule et al., 'Biodiversity, extinction, and humanity's future'.

72 J. Rockström et al., 'A safe operating space for humanity', *Nature* 461(7263), 2009: 472–5.

73 Will Steffen et al., 'Planetary boundaries: Guiding human development on a changing planet', *Science* 347(6223), http://precaution . org / lib / steffen _ planetary _ boundaries(incl_supple mental).150213.pdf.

74 D. E. Canfield et al., 'The evolution and future of Earth's nitrogen cycle', *Science* 330(6001), 2010: 192–6.

75 V. H. Smith et al., 'Eutrophication of freshwater and marine ecosystems', *Limnology and Oceanography* 51(1), 2006: 351–5.

76 J. Rockström et al., 'Planetary boundaries: Exploring the safe operating space for humanity', *Ecology and Society* 14(2), 2009: 32.

77 T. Gleeson et al., 'Water balance of global aquifers revealed by groundwater footprint', *Nature* 488, 2012: 197–200. In the United States, China and India, 70 per cent of subterranean water is used for agriculture. See M. W. Rosegrant et al., 'Water for agriculture: maintaining food security under growing scarcity', *Annual Review of Environment and Resources* 34, 2009: 205–22.

78 C. J. Vörösmarty et al., 'Global threats to human water security and river biodiversity', *Nature* 467, 2010: 555–61.

79 In spite of technologies that hide the real cause for the exhaustion of resources.

80 André Cicolella, *Toxique Planète* (Paris: Seuil, 2013); F. Nicolino, *Un empoisonnement universel. Comment les produits chimiques ont envahi la planète* (Paris: Les Liens qui Libèrent, 2013).

81 N. Vandenberg et al., *Endocrine Reviews* 33, 378, 2012, quoted in L. J. Guillette and T. Iguchi, 'Life in a contaminated world', *Science* 337, 2012: 1614–15.

82 For example 'experts at the TFSP [Consortium] note that imidaclopride has been detected in 91 per cent of 74 samples of French soil analysed in 2005: only 15 per cent of the sites had been treated . . .', quoted in Foucart, 'Le déclin massif des insectes'.

83 L. U. Chensheng et al., 'Sub-lethal exposure to neonicotinoids impaired honey bees' winterization before proceeding to colony collapse disorder', *Bulletin of Insectology* 67(1), 2014: 125–30.

84 D. Gibbons et al., 'A review of the direct and indirect effects of neonicotinoids and fipronil on vertebrate wildlife', *Environmental Science and Pollution Research*, 2014: 1–16.

85 J. P. Van der Sluijs et al., 'Conclusions of the Worldwide Integrated Assessment on the risks of neonicotinoids and fipronil to biodiversity and ecosystem functioning', *Environmental Science and Pollution Research* 22(1), 2014: 148–54.

86 Sophie Landrin and Laetitia Van Eeckhout, 'La pollution à Paris aussi nocive que le tabagisme passif', *Le Monde*, 24 November 2014.

87 M. Scheffer et al., 'Catastrophic shifts in ecosystems', *Nature* 413(6856), 2001: 591–6.

88 S. Kefi et al., 'Spatial vegetation patterns and imminent desertification in Mediterranean arid ecosystems', *Nature* 449(7159), 2007: 213–17.

89 J. A. Foley et al., 'Regime shifts in the Sahara and Sahel: Interactions between ecological and climatic systems in Northern Africa', *Ecosystems* 6(6), 2003: 524–32.

90 E. A. Davidson et al., 'The Amazon basin in transition', *Nature* 481, 2012: 321–8.

91 T. M. Lenton et al., 'Tipping elements in the Earth's climate system', *Proceedings of the National Academy of Sciences* 105(6), 2008: 1786–93.

92 T. M. Lenton, 'Arctic climate tipping points', *Ambio* 41(1), 2012: 10–22.

93 A. P. Kinzig et al., 'Resilience and regime shifts: Assessing cascading effects', *Ecology and Society* 11, 2006: 20; Malcolm Gladwell, *The Tipping Point: How Little Things Can Make a Big Difference* (New York: Little, Brown and Co., 2000); B. Hunter, 'Tipping points in social networks', Stanford University Symbolic Systems Course Blog, 2012.

94 D. Korowicz, 'Trade Off: Financial system supply-chain cross contagion – a study in global systemic collapse', FEASTA, 2012, http://www.feasta.org/wp-content/uploads/2012/10/Trade_Off_Korowicz.pdf.

95 A. D. Barnosky et al., 'Approaching a state shift in Earth's biosphere', *Nature* 486, 2012: 52–8.

96 Audrey Garric, 'La fin de la planète en 2100?', Le Monde Blog Eco(lo), 27 July 2012, https://www.lemonde.fr/planete/article/2012/07/27/la-fin-de-la-planete-en-2100_5982078_3244.html.

97 T. P. Hughes et al., 'Multiscale regime shifts and planetary boundaries', *Trends in Ecology & Evolution* 28(7), 2013: 389–95.

98 B. W. Brook et al., 'Does the terrestrial biosphere have planetary tipping points?', *Trends in Ecology & Evolution* 28(7), 2013: 396–401.

Chapter 4 Is the Steering Locked?

1 P. A. David, 'Clio and the Economics of QWERTY', *The American Economic Review* 25(2), 1985: 332–7.
2 Charles Herve-Gruyer and Perrine Herve-Gruyer, *Permaculture. Guérir la terre, nourrir les hommes* (Arles: Actes Sud, 2014).
3 O. De Schutter and G. Vanloqueren, 'The new green revolution: How twenty-first-century science can feed the world', *Solutions* 2(4), 2011: 33–44.
4 http://www.rightlivelihood.org/gao.html.
5 O. De Schutter et al., 'Agroécologie et droit à l'alimentation', report to the 16th session of the UN Council of Human Rights, 2011 (A/HRC/16/49).
6 FAO, International Symposium on Agroecology for Food Security and Nutrition, Rome, 18–19 September 2014, http://www.fao.org/about/meetings/afns/en/.
7 G. C. Unruh, 'Understanding carbon lock-in', *Energy Policy* 28(12), 2000: 817–30.
8 Bonneuil and Fressoz, *L'Événement Anthropocène*, pp. 129–33.
9 M. A. Janssen and M. Scheffer, 'Overexploitation of renewable resources by ancient societies and the role of sunk-cost effects', *Ecology and Society* 9(1), 2004: 6.
10 International Energy Agency, *World Energy Outlook 2014*.
11 Robert-Vincent Joule and Jean-Léon Beauvois, *Petit traité de manipulation à l'usage des honnêtes gens* (Grenoble: Presses universitaires de Grenoble, 2009).
12 G. Vanloqueren and P. V. Baret, 'How agricultural research systems shape a technological regime that develops genetic engineering but locks out agroecological innovations', *Research Policy* 38(6), 2009: 971–83; G. Vanloqueren and P. V. Baret, 'Why are ecological, low-input, multi-resistant wheat cultivars slow to develop commercially? A Belgian agricultural "lock-in" case study', *Ecological Economics* 66(2), 2008: 436–46.
13 J. Gadrey, 'La "démocratie écologique" de Dominique Bourg n'est pas la solution', *Alternatives économiques*, 18 January 2011.
14 Adam Rome, 2001. Quoted in J.-B. Fressoz, 'Pour une histoire désorientée de l'énergie', *Entropia. Revue d'étude théorique et politique de la décroissance* 15, 2013.

15 F. Veillerette and F. Nicolino, *Pesticides, révélations sur un scandale français* (Paris: Fayard, 2007).

16 See the video, 'DDT so safe you can eat it 1947', available at www.youtube.com/watch?v=gtcXXbuR244.

17 M. Scheffer et al., 'Slow response of societies to new problems: Causes and costs', *Ecosystems* 6(5), 2003: 493–502.

18 Joseph A. Tainter, *The Collapse of Complex Societies* (Cambridge, UK: Cambridge University Press, 2013 [1988]).

19 G. C. Unruh and J. Carrillo-Hermosilla, 'Globalizing carbon lock-in', *Energy Policy* 34(10), 2006: 1185–97.

20 P. Gai et al., 'Complexity, concentration and contagion', *Journal of Monetary Economics* 58(5), 2011: 453–70.

21 S. Vitali et al., 'The network of global corporate control', *PloS ONE* 6(10), 2011: e25995.

22 Bonneuil and Fressoz, *L'Événement Anthropocène*, p. 129.

23 Richard Heede, 'Tracing anthropogenic carbon dioxide and methane emissions to fossil fuel and cement producers, 1854–2010', *Climatic Change* 122, 2014: 229–41.

24 Richard Douthwaite, *The Growth Illusion: How Economic Growth Has Enriched the Few, Impoverished the Many and Endangered the Planet* (Foxhole, Dartington: Green Books, 1999).

25 Quoted by A. Miller and R. Hopkins, 'Climate after growth: Why environmentalists must embrace post-growth economics and community resilience', Post-Carbon Institute, September 2013.

26 David Holmgren, 'Crash on demand. Welcome to the brown tech world', *Holmgren Design*, December 2013.

Chapter 5 Trapped in an Ever More Fragile Vehicle

1 D. Arkell, 'The evolution of creation', *Boeing Frontiers Online* 3(10), 2005, http://www.boeing.com/news/frontiers/archive/2005/march/mainfeature1.html.

2 Quoted in Debora MacKenzie, 'Why the demise of civilisation may be inevitable', *New Scientist* 2650, 2008: 32–5.

3 MacKenzie, 'Why the demise of civilisation may be inevitable'.

4 Ian Goldin and Mike Mariathasan, *The Butterfly Defect: How Globalization Creates Systemic Risks, and What to Do about It* (Princeton, NJ: Princeton University Press, 2014).

5 Robert M. May et al., 'Complex systems: Ecology for bankers', *Nature* 451(7181), 2008: 893–5.

6 Andrew G. Haldane and Vasileios Madouros, 'The dog and the frisbee', in speech at the Federal Reserve Bank of Kansas City's Jackson Hole economic policy symposium, Jackson Hole, Wyoming, USA, 31 August 2012.

7 Michael Lewis, *Flash Boys: A Wall Street Revolt* (New York: W. W. Norton & Company, 2014).

8 Bank of International Settlements, 'OTC derivatives market activity in the second half of 2013', 8 May 2014, http://www.bis.org/publ/otc_hy1405.htm.

9 Gai et al. 'Complexity, concentration and contagion'.

10 P. Gai and S. Kapadia, 'Contagion in financial networks', *Proceedings of the Royal Society A* 466(2120), 2010: 2401–23.

11 R. J. Caballero and A. Simsek, 'Fire sales in a model of complexity', *The Journal of Finance* 68(6), 2013: 2549–87.

12 E. Yardeni and M. Quitana, 'Global economic briefing: Central Bank balance sheets', Yardeni Research Inc., December 2014.

13 Jonathan Soble, 'Japan abruptly acts to stimulate economy', *The New York Times*, 31 October 2014.

14 John Maynard Keynes, *The Economic Consequences of the Peace* (New York: Skyhorse Publishing, 2007 [1919]), p. 134.

15 Eurostat, 'General Government Gross Debt – Annual Data', http://ec.europa.eu/eurostat/tgm/table.do?tab=table&init=1&language=en&pcode=teina225.

16 Thomas Vampouille, 'Les stocks stratégiques pétroliers en France', *Le Figaro*, 28 March 2012.

17 World Economic Forum, 'Impact of Thailand Floods 2011 on supply chain', Mimeo, WEF, 2012, p. 18, https://www.econstor.eu/bitstream/10419/64267/1/717874087.pdf.

18 White House, 'National strategy for global supply chain security', Washington, DC, 2012, p. 4, https://obamawhitehouse.archives.gov/sites/default/files/national_strategy_for_global_supply_chain_security.pdf.

19 Quoted by Simon Cox, 'US food supply vulnerable to attack', BBC Radio 4, 22 August 2006, http://news.bbc.co.uk/1/hi/world/americas/5274022.stm.

20 L. M. Wein and Y. Liu, 'Analyzing a bioterror attack on the food supply: The case of botulinum toxin in milk', *Proceedings*

of the National Academy of Sciences of the United States of America 102(28), 2005: 9984–9.

21 H. Escaith, 'Trade collapse, trade relapse and global production networks: Supply chains in the great recession', MPRA Paper no. 18274, OECD Roundtable on impacts of the economic crisis on globalization and global value chains, Paris, 28 October 2009; H. Escaith et al., 'International supply chains and trade elasticity in times of global crisis', World Trade Organization (Economic Research and Statistics Division), 2010, Staff Working Paper ERSD-2010-08.

22 K. J. Mizgier et al., 'Modeling defaults of companies In multi-stage supply chain networks', *International Journal of Production Economics* 135(1), 2012: 14–23; S. Battiston et al., 'Credit chains and bankruptcy propagation in production networks', *Journal of Economic Dynamics and Control* 31(6), 2007: 2061–84.

23 Andrew G. Haldane and Robert M. May, 'Systemic risk in banking ecosystems', *Nature* 469(7330), 2011: 351–5.

24 SWIFT (Society for Worldwide Interbank Financial Tele-communication), http://www.swift.com/about_swift/company_information/company_information.

25 Oxford Economics, *The Economic Impacts of Air Travel Restrictions Due to Volcanic Ash* (Oxford: Abbey House, 2010).

26 N. Robinson, 'The politics of the fuel protests: Towards a multi-dimensional explanation', *The Political Quarterly* 73(1), 2002: 58–66.

27 Alan McKinnon, 'Life without trucks: The impact of a temporary disruption of road freight transport on a national economy', *Journal of Business Logistics* 27(2), 2006: 227–50.

28 R. D. Holcomb, 'When trucks stop, America stops', American Trucking Association, 2006.

29 Debora MacKenzie, 'Will a pandemic bring down civilisation?', *New Scientist*, 5 April 2008.

30 H. Byrd and S. Matthewman, 'Exergy and the city: The technology and sociology of power (failure)', *Journal of Urban Technology* 21(3), 2014: 85–102.

31 Goldin and Mariathasan, *The Butterfly Defect*, p. 101.

32 Steve Kroft, 'Falling apart: America's neglected infrastructure', *CBS News*, 23 November 2014, http://www.cbsnews.com/news/falling-apart-america-neglected-infrastructure/.

33 Kroft, 'Falling apart'.
34 Korowicz, 'Trade-Off: Financial system supply-chain cross contagion'.
35 MacKenzie, 'Will a pandemic bring down civilisation?'
36 MacKenzie, 'Will a pandemic bring down civilisation?'
37 Quoted in MacKenzie, 'Will a pandemic bring down civilisation?'
38 MacKenzie, 'Will a pandemic bring down civilisation?'
39 Ian Goldin, *Divided Nations: Why Global Governance is Failing, and What We Can Do About It* (Oxford: Oxford University Press, 2013).
40 B. Walker et al., 'Looming global-scale failures and missing institutions', *Science* 325(5946), 2009: 1345–6.
41 D. Helbing, 'Globally networked risks and how to respond', *Nature* 497(7447), 2013: 51–9.

Summary of Part I

1 'L'ONU estime qu'un million de personnes sont menacées par la faim à cause d'Ebola', LeMonde.fr, 17 December 2014.
2 Rémi Barroux, 'Ebola met à mal tout le système de santé guinéen', *Le Monde*, 31 December 2014.
3 Phosphates are used mainly as fertilizers.

Chapter 6 The Difficulties of Being a Futurologist

1 A. B. Frank et al., 'Dealing with femtorisks in international relations', *PNAS* 111(49), 2014: 17356–62.
2 Paul R. Ehrlich, *The Population Bomb* (New York: Ballantine Books, 1968).
3 Rachel Carson, *Silent Spring* (Boston, MA: Houghton Mifflin, 1962).
4 D. Nuccitelli, 'A remarkably accurate global warming prediction, made in 1972', *The Guardian*, 19 March 2014.
5 A. Kilpatrick and A. Marm, 'Globalization, land use, and the invasion of West Nile virus', *Science* 334(6054), 2011: 323–7.
6 Nassim Nicholas Taleb, *The Black Swan: The Impact of the Highly Improbable* (New York: Random House, 2007).
7 Quoted in Jean-Pierre Dupuy, *Pour un catastrophisme éclairé*, p. 105.

8 Dupuy, *Pour un catastrophisme éclairé*, pp. 84–5.

9 D. J. Snowden and M. E. Boone, 'A leader's framework for decision making', *Harvard Business Review* 85(11), 2007: 59–69.

10 Dupuy, *Pour un catastrophisme éclairé*, p. 13.

11 Hans Jonas, quoted by Dupuy, *Pour un catastrophisme éclairé*.

12 Dupuy, *Pour un catastrophisme éclairé*, p. 63.

13 Dupuy, *Pour un catastrophisme éclairé*, pp. 84–5.

Chapter 7 Can We Detect Warning Signs?

1 S. Kéfi et al., 'Spatial vegetation patterns and imminent desertification in Mediterranean arid ecosystems', *Nature* 449(7159), 2007: 213–17.

2 L. Dai et al., 'Slower recovery in space before collapse of connected populations', *Nature* 496(7445), 2013: 355–8.

3 S. Carpenter et al., 'Early warnings of regime shifts: A whole-ecosystem experiment', *Science* 332(6033), 2011: 1079–82; A. J. Veraart et al., 'Recovery rates reflect distance to a tipping point in a living system', *Nature* 481(7381), 2012: 357–9; L. Dai et al., 'Generic indicators for loss of resilience before a tipping point leading to population collapse', *Science* 336(6085), 2012: 1175–7.

4 C. A. Boulton et al., 'Early warning signals of Atlantic Meridional Overturning Circulation collapse in a fully coupled climate model', *Nature Communications* 5 (752), 2014.

5 T. Lenton et al., 'Tipping elements in the Earth's climate system', *Proceedings of the National Academy of Sciences* 105(6), 2008: 1786–93.

6 R. Wang et al., 'Flickering gives early warning signals of a critical transition to a eutrophic lake state', *Nature* 4929(7429), 2012: 419–22.

7 Veraart et al., 'Recovery rates reflect distance to a tipping point'.

8 J. Bascompte and P. Jordano, 'Plant-animal mutualistic networks: The architecture of biodiversity', *Annual Review of Ecology, Evolution, and Systematics* 38, 2007: 567–93.

9 M. Scheffer et al., 'Anticipating critical transitions', *Science* 338(6105), 2012: 344–8.

10 Robert M. May et al., 'Complex systems: Ecology for bankers', *Nature* 451(7181), 2008: 893–5.

11 Igor Klopotan, Jovan Zoroja and Maja Meško, 'Early warning system in business, finance, and economics: Bibliometric and topic analysis', *International Journal of Engineering Business Management* 10(5), 2018. https://journals.sagepub.com/doi/pdf/10.1177/1847979018797013.

12 M. Gallegati, 'Early warning signals of financial stress: A "wavelet-based" composite indicators approach', in *Advances in Non-linear Economic Modeling* (Berlin-Heidelberg: Springer, 2014), pp. 115–38; R. Quax et al., 'Information dissipation as an early-warning signal for the Lehman Brothers collapse in financial time series', *Scientific Reports* 3, 30 May 2013.

13 V. Dakos et al., 'Resilience indicators: prospects and limitations for early warnings of regime shifts', *Philosophical Transactions of the Royal Society B: Biological Sciences* 370(1659), 2015: 20130263.

14 S. R. Carpenter et al., 'A new approach for rapid detection of nearby thresholds in ecosystem time series', *Oikos* 123(3), 2014: 290–7.

15 S. Kéfi et al., 'Early warning signals also precede non-catastrophic transitions', *Oikos*, 122(5), 2013: 641–8.

16 Institute of Chartered Accountants in Australia, 'Early warning systems'.

17 Dupuy, *Pour un catastrophisme éclairé*, p. 132.

Chapter 8 What Do the Mathematical Models Say?

1 S. Motesharrei et al., 'Human and nature dynamics (HANDY): Modeling inequality and use of resources in the collapse or sustainability of societies', *Ecological Economics* 101, 2014: 90–102.

2 Hervé Kempf, *How the Rich are Destroying the Earth* (Foxhole, Dartington: Green Books, 2008).

3 Joseph Stiglitz, *The Price of Inequality. How Today's Divided Society Endangers Our Future* (New York: W. W. Norton and Company, 2012), p. 14.

4 Richard Wilkinson and Kate Pickett, *The Spirit Level: Why More Equal Societies Almost Always Do Better* (London: Allen Lane, 2009).

5 Stewart Lansley, *The Cost of Inequality: Three Decades of the Super-Rich and the Economy* (London: Gibson Square Books, 2011).

6 C. B. Field et al., 'Climate change 2014: Impacts, adaptation, and vulnerability', Contribution of Working Group II to the Fifth Assessment Report of the Intergovernmental Panel on Climate Change (IPCC), 2014.

7 Thomas Piketty, *Capital in the Twenty-First Century*, trans. Arthur Goldhammer (Boston, MA: Harvard University Press, 2014).

8 See E. Marshall, 'Tax man's gloomy message: The rich will get richer', *Science* 344(6186), 2014: 826–7.

9 E. Saez and G. Zucman, 'Wealth inequality in the United States since 1913: Evidence from capitalized income Tax Data', Working Paper, National Bureau of Economic Research, 2014, http://www.nber.org/papers/w20625.

10 Motesharrei et al., 'Human and nature dynamics (HANDY)', p. 100.

11 Donella Meadows et al., *Limits to Growth: The 30-Year Update* (White River Junction VT: Chelsea Green Publishing, 1992).

12 A group bringing together scientists, economists, national and international civil servants as well as industrialists from fifty-three countries.

13 Meadows et al., *Beyond the Limits: Global Collapse or a Sustainable Future* (New York: Earthscan Publications, 1992).

14 Meadows et al., *Limits to Growth*.

15 G. M. Turner, 'A comparison of *The Limits to Growth* with 30 years of reality', *Global Environmental Change* 18(3), 2008: 397–411; G. M. Turner, 'On the cusp of global collapse? Updated comparison of *The Limits to Growth* with historical data', *GAIA-Ecological Perspectives for Science and Society* 21(2), 2012: 116–24.

16 As well as the interviews published in *Le Monde*, *Libération*, *Imagine* and *Terra Eco*, see his article 'Il est trop tard pour le développement durable', in Agnès Sinaï (ed.), *Penser la décroissance. Politiques de l'Anthropocène* (Paris: Les Presses de Sciences-Po, 'Nouveaux Débats', 2013), pp. 195–210.

Chapter 9 A Mosaic to Explore

1 *Dictionnaire Littré* , online (XMLittré v2), www.littre.org.

2 Jared Diamond, *Collapse: How Societies Choose to Fail or Survive* (London: Penguin, 2006), p. 13.

3 Pierre Clastres, *La Société contre l'État* (Paris: Minuit, 2011); James C. Scott, *The Art of Not Being Governed: An Anarchist History of Upland Southeast Asia* (New Haven, CT: Yale University Press, 2009).

4 Peter Kropotkin, *Mutual Aid: A Factor of Evolution* (New York: McLure Phillips & Co., 1902).

5 Naomi Oreskes and Erik M. Conway, *The Collapse of Western Civilization: A View from the Future* (New York: Columbia University Press, 2014).

6 John Michael Greer, *The Long Descent: A User's Guide to the End of the Industrial Age* (Gabriola Island, BC, Canada: New Society Publishers, 2008).

7 Serge Latouche, *Le Pari de la décroissance* (Paris: Fayard, 2006).

8 Peter Turchin, *Historical Dynamics: Why States Rise and Fall* (Princeton, NJ: Princeton University Press, 2003); Peter Turchin, *War and Peace and War: The Rise and Fall of Empires* (London: Penguin Group, 2007); Peter Turchin and Sergey Nefedov, *Secular Cycles* (Princeton: Princeton University Press, 2009).

9 Bryan Ward-Perkins, *The Fall of Rome and the End of Civilization* (Oxford: Oxford University Press, 2005).

10 K. W. Butzer, 'Collapse, environment, and society', *PNAS* 109(10), 2012: 3632–9.

11 Virginie Duvat and Alexandre Magnan, *Des catastrophes . . . 'naturelles'?* (Paris: Le Pommier, 2014).

12 William Ophuls, *Immoderate Greatness: Why Civilizations Fail* (North Charleston, SC: CreateSpace Independent Publishing Platform, 2012), p. 63.

13 Turchin and Nefedov, *Secular Cycles*.

14 Butzer, 'Collapse, environment, and society'.

15 D. Biggs et al., 'Are we entering an era of concatenated global crises?', *Ecology and Society* 16(2), 2011: 27–37.

16 Dmitry Orlov, *Reinventing Collapse: The Soviet Experience and American Prospects* (Gabriola Island, BC, Canada: New Society Publishers, 2008). See also his excellent blog: http://cluborlov.blogspot.com.

17 Dmitry Orlov, *The Five Stages of Collapse: Survivors' Toolkit* (Gabriola Island, BC, Canada: New Society Publishers, 2013).

18 Orlov, *The Five Stages of Collapse*, p. 14.

19 Orlov, *The Five Stages of Collapse*, p. 14.

20 Orlov, *The Five Stages of Collapse*, p. 15.

21 Orlov, *The Five Stages of Collapse*, p. 15.

22 Orlov, *The Five Stages of Collapse*, p. 15.

23 Dmitry Orlov, 'The sixth stage of collapse', ClubOrlov, 22 October 2013, http://cluborlov.blogspot.be/2013/10/the-sixth-stage-of-collapse.html.

24 Lance H. Gunderson and C. S. Holling (eds), *Panarchy: Understanding Transformations in Human and Natural Systems* (Washington, Covelo, London: Island Press, 2002).

25 David Korowicz, *Tipping Point: Near-Term Systemic Implications of a Peak in Global Oil Production. An Outline Review*, FEASTA & The Risk/Resilience Network, 2010, available online at https://www.feasta.org/2010/03/15/tipping-point-near-term-systemic-impli cations-of-a-peak-in-global-oil-production-an-outline-review/.

26 Greer, *The Long Descent*.

27 See also the third model presented in Yves Cochet, 'Les trois modèles du monde', in Agnès Sinaï (ed.), *Penser la décroissance. Politiques de l'Anthropocène* (Paris: Les Presses de Sciences-Po, 'Nouveaux Débats', 2013), pp. 62–71.

28 See the work of Emmanuel Wallerstein, especially *The Modern World-System, Vol. I: Capitalist Agriculture and the Origins of the European World-Economy in the Sixteenth Century* (New York and London: Academic Press, 1974) and subsequent volumes.

29 G. D. Kuecker and T. D. Hall, 'Resilience and community in the age of World-system collapse', *Nature and Culture* 6, 2011: 1840.

30 O. De Schutter et al., 'Agroécologie et droit à l'alimentation', report to the 16th session of the UN Council of Human Rights, 2011 (A/HRC/16/49).

31 DEFRA, 'UK Food Security Assessment: Detailed Analysis', 2010. https://webarchive.nationalarchives.gov.uk/201304021912 30/http:/archive.defra.gov.uk/foodfarm/food/pdf/food-assess100 105.pdf.

32 David Korowicz, 'On the cusp of collapse: Complexity, energy and the globalised economy', in *Fleeing Vesuvius. Overcoming the Risks of Economic and Environmental Collapse* (FEASTA & New Society Publishers, 2010), http://fleeingvesuvius.org/2011/10/08/on-the-cusp-of-collapse-complexity-energy-and-the-globalised-economy/.

33 'Rusting brakes: Germany faces freight train shortage as growth picks up', *Spiegel Online*, 5 April 2010, http://www.spiegel.de/international/business/rusting-brakes-germany-faces-freight-train-shortage-as-growth-picks-up-a-687291.html.

34 M. Derex et al., 'Experimental evidence for the influence of group size on cultural complexity', *Nature* 503(7476), 2013: 389–91.

35 Derex et al., 'Experimental evidence', p. 391.

36 'Le déclin du nucléaire', interview with Mycle Schneider, *Silence* 410, 2013: 5–9.

37 Schneider, 'Le déclin du nucléaire'.

38 R. Heinberg and J. Mander, *Searching for a Miracle: Net Energy Limits and the Fate of Industrial Society*, Post-Carbon Institute, 2009, p. 37, available online at https://www.postcarbon.org/publications/searching-for-a-miracle/.

39 For more details on this problematic, see Pablo Servigne, 'Le nucléaire pour l'après-pétrole?', *Barricade*, 2014. Available at www.barricade.be.

Chapter 10 And Where Do Human Beings Fit into All This?

1 M. Sourrouille (ed.), *Moins nombreux, plus heureux. L'urgence écologique de repenser la démographie* (Paris: Sang de la Terre, 2014).

2 P. Gerland et al., 'World population stabilization unlikely this century', *Science* 346(6206) 2014: 234–7.

3 Ester Boserup, *Évolution agraire et pression démographique* (Paris: Flammarion, 1970).

4 Hugues Stockael, *La Faim du monde* (Paris: Max Milo, 2012).

5 Vaclav Smil, *Enriching the Earth: Fritz Haber, Carl Bosch, and the Transformation of World Food Production* (Boston, MA: MIT Press, 2004); N. Gruber and J. N. Galloway, 'An Earth System perspective of the global nitrogen cycle', *Nature* 451, 2008: 293–6.

6 P. Rasmont and S. Vray, 'Les crises alimentaires en Belgique au XXIe siècle', *Les Cahiers nouveaux* 85, 2013: 47–50.

7 G. C. Daily and Paul R. Ehrlich, 'Population, sustainability, and Earth's carrying capacity', *BioScience*, 1992: 761–71.

8 Also known as Jevons' Paradox: the introduction of a more efficient technology into the use of a resource increases the consumption of that resource instead of lessening it.

9 Harald Welzer, *Les Guerres du climat. Pourquoi on tue au XXIe siècle* (Paris: Gallimard, 2009).

10 IPCC, 'Summary for Policymakers', in *Climate Change 2014: Impacts, Adaptation, and Vulnerability. Part A: Global and Sectoral Aspects. Contribution of Working Group II to the Fifth Assessment Report of the Intergovernmental Panel on Climate Change* (Cambridge and New York: Cambridge University Press, pp. 1–32).

11 S. M. Hsiang, M. Burke and E. Miguel, 'Quantifying the influence of climate on human conflict', *Science* 341(6151), 2013: 1235367.

12 J. O' Loughlin et al., 'Modeling and data choices sway conclusions about climate-conflict links', *PNAS* 111, 2014: 2054–5.

13 J. Scheffran and A. Battaglini, 'Climate and conflicts: The security risks of global warming', *Regional Environmental Change* 11(1), 2011: 27–39.

14 Nafeez Ahmed, 'Pentagon preparing for mass civil breakdown', *The Guardian*, 12 June 2014; Nafeez Ahmed 'Pentagon bracing for public dissent over climate and energy shocks', *The Guardian*, 14 June 2013.

15 Daniel P. Aldrich, *Building Resilience: Social Capital in Post-Disaster Recovery* (Chicago, IL: University of Chicago Press, 2012).

16 Rebecca Solnit, *A Paradise Built in Hell: The Extraordinary Communities That Arise in Disaster* (London: Penguin Books, 2012).

17 Quoted in Jacques Lecomte, *La Bonté humaine. Altruisme, empathie, générosité* (Odile Jacob: Paris, 2012), p. 24. See also https://www.theguardian.com/world/2005/sep/06/hurricanekatrina.usa3.

18 L. Clarke, 'Panic: myth or reality?', *Contexts* 1(3), 2002: 21–6.

19 R. Olshansky, 'San Francisco, Kobe, New Orleans: Lessons for rebuilding', *Social Policy* 36(2), 2006: 17–19.

20 For example, D. Helbing and W. Yu, 'The outbreak of cooperation among success-driven individuals under noisy conditions', *PNAS* 106(10), 2009: 3680–5.

21 Lecomte, *La Bonté humaine*.

22 J.-M. Jancovici, 'Combien suis-je un esclavagiste?', *Manicore*, 2013, www.manicore.com/documentation/esclaves.html.

23 Samuel Bowles and Herbert Gintis, *A Cooperative Species: Human*

Reciprocity and Its Evolution (Princeton, NJ: Princeton University Press, 2011).

24 This phenomenon is commonly found in disaster movies, especially those dealing with plane crashes, as well as in most zombie films. For braver readers, see L. Clarke, 'Panic: myth or reality?', *Contexts* 1(3), 2002: 21–6.

25 B. E. Goldstein et al., 'Narrating resilience: Transforming urban systems through collaborative storytelling', in 'Special issue: Governing for urban resilience', *Urban Studies*, 2013: 1–17.

26 Serge Latouche, *Décoloniser l'imaginaire: la pensée creative contre l'économie de l'absurde* (Paris: Parangon, 2011).

27 'Transition tales' are activities set up by transition initiatives to make primary and secondary school children aware of the two-fold challenge of the oil peak and climate change by imagining solutions based on positive stories.

28 Luc Semal, 'Politiques locales de décroissance', in Agnès Sinaï (ed.), *Penser la décroissance*, p. 157.

29 See the articles by Pablo Servigne, 'Au-delà du vote "démocratique". Les nouveaux modes de gouvernance', and 'Outils de facilitation et techniques d'intelligence collective', published by *Barricade* in 2011. Available online at www.barricade.be.

30 Clive Hamilton, *Requiem for a Species: Why We Resist the Truth about Climate Change* (New York: Earthscan Publications, 2010).

31 Craig Dilworth, *Too Smart for Our Own Good: The Ecological Predicament of Humankind* (Cambridge: Cambridge University Press, 2010).

32 Cited in Greg Harman, 'Your brain on climate change: Why the threat produces apathy, not action', *The Guardian*, 10 November 2014. https://www.theguardian.com/sustainable-business/2014/nov/10/brain-climate-change-science-psychology-environment-elections.

33 Hamilton, *Requiem for a Species*, p. 120.

34 Callum Roberts, *Ocean of Life* (London: Penguin, 2013), p. 41.

35 Dennis Meadows, 'Il est trop tard pour le développement durable', in Agnès Sinaï (ed.), *Penser la décroissance. Politiques de l'Anthropocène* (Paris: Les Presses de Sciences-Po, 'Nouveaux Débats', 2013), pp. 195–210, p. 199.

36 Jean-Pierre Dupuy, *Pour un catastrophisme éclairé: quand l'impossible est certain* (Paris: Seuil, 2002), p. 142.

37 Meadows, 'Il est trop tard', p. 204.

38 Meadows, 'Il est trop tard', p. 203.

39 Meadows, 'Il est trop tard', p. 203.

40 Naomi Oreskes and Eric M. Conway, *Merchants of Doubt. How a Handful of Scientists Obscured the Truth on Issues from Tobacco Smoke to Global Warming* (London: Bloomsbury, 2010); Stéphane Foucart, *La Fabrique du mensonge: comment les industriels manipulent la science et nous mettent en danger* (Paris: Denoël, 2013).

41 Oreskes and Conway, *Merchants of Doubt*, p. 16.

42 K. Brysse et al., 'Climate change prediction: Erring on the side of least drama?', *Global Environmental Change* 23(1): 327–37.

43 Hamilton, *Requiem for a Species*, pp. xi–xii.

44 Hamilton, *Requiem for a Species*, p. xii.

45 S. C. Moser and L. Dilling, 'Toward the social tipping point: Creating a climate for change', in *Creating a Climate for Change: Communicating Climate Change and Facilitating Social Change* (Cambridge: Cambridge University Press, 2007), pp. 491–516; M. Milinski et al., 'The collective-risk social dilemma and the prevention of simulated dangerous climate change', *PNAS* 105, 2008: 2291–4.

46 David Servan-Schreiber, *Anticancer: A New Way of Life* (London: Penguin, 2008).

47 Hamilton, *Requiem for a Species*, p. xiv.

48 Hamilton, *Requiem for a Species*, p. x.

49 Hamilton, *Requiem for a Species*, p. x.

50 Hamilton, *Requiem for a Species*; Joanna Macy, *Écopsychologie pratique et rituels pour la Terre. Retrouver le lien vivant avec la nature* (Paris: Le Souffle d'Or, 2008); Bill Plotkin, *Nature and the Human Soul: Cultivating Wholeness in a Fragmented World* (Novato, CA: New World Library, 2008); Carolyn Baker, *Navigating the Coming Chaos: A Handbook for Inner Transition* (Bloomington, IN: iUniverse, 2011).

51 See, for example, the website of Terr'Eveille, www.terreveille.be.

52 Hamilton, *Requiem for a Species*, p. xiii.

53 D. J. F. de Quervain et al., 'The neural basis of altruistic punishment', *Science* 305, 2004: 1254–8.

54 Comité invisible, *L'Insurrection qui vient* (Paris: La Fabrique, 2007); Comité invisible, *À nos amis* (Paris: La Fabrique, 2014).

55 *Silence, Imagine, Bastamag, La Décroissance* and *Passerelle Éco.*

56 Rob Hopkins, *The Power of Just Doing Stuff: How Local Action Can Change the World* (Totnes: Green, 2013); Bénédicte Manier, *Un million de révolutions tranquilles* (Paris: Les Liens qui Libèrent, 2012).

57 Semal, 'Politiques locales de décroissance', p. 144.

58 Rob Hopkins, *The Transition Companion: Making Your Community More Resilient in Uncertain Times* (White River Junction VT: Chelsea Green Publishing Company, 2011).

59 B. Thévard, 'Vers des territoires résilients', study produced for the group Les Verts/ALE au Parlement européen, 2014; Rob Hopkins, *The Transition Handbook: From Oil Dependency to Local Resilience* (Totnes: Green, 2008).

60 Agnès Sinaï (ed.), *Économie de l'après-croissance. Politiques de l'Anthropocène II*, (Paris: Presses de Sciences Po, 2015); John Michael Greer, 'The World After Abundance', available online at: https://www.countercurrents.org/greer280510.htm.

61 Jared Diamond, *Collapse: How Societies Choose to Fail or Survive* (London: Penguin, 2006), pp. 296ff.

62 A. Canabate, 'La cohésion sociale en temps de récession prolongée. Espagne, Grèce, Portugal', study produced for the Greens/European Free in the European Parliament, 2014.

63 A. Miller and R. Hopkins, 'Climate after growth: Why environmentalists must embrace post-growth economics and community resilience', Post-Carbon Institute, September 2013, p. 9, note.

64 David Holmgren, 'Crash on demand: Welcome to the brown tech world', *Holmgren Design*, December 2013.

65 Pablo Servigne and Christian Araud, 'La transition inachevée. Cuba et l'après-pétrole', *Barricade*, 2012, available online at www.barricade.be.

66 Mike Davis, 'Écologie en temps de guerre. Quand les États-Unis luttaient contre le gaspillage des ressources', *Mouvements* 54, 2008: 93–8.

67 M. Szuba, 'Régimes de justice énergétique', in Sinaï (ed.), *Penser la décroissance*, p. 132.

68 Szuba, 'Régimes de justice énergétique', p. 120.

69 Szuba, 'Régimes de justice énergétique', pp. 134–5.
70 Szuba, 'Régimes de justice énergétique', p. 136.
71 Michel Rocard et al., 'Le genre humain, menacé', *Le Monde*, 2 April 2011.
72 Naomi Klein, *The Shock Doctrine: The Rise of Disaster Capitalism* (London: Penguin, 2008).
73 Hervé Kempf, *L'Oligarchie ça suffit, vive la démocratie* (Paris: Seuil, 2011).
74 Semal, 'Politiques locales de décroissance', p. 147.

Conclusion

1 Paul R. Ehrlich and Anne H. Ehrlich, 'Can a collapse of global civilization be avoided?', *Philosophical Transactions of the Royal Society B* 280(1754), 2013: 20122845.
2 Clive Hamilton, *Requiem for a Species: Why We Resist the Truth about Climate Change* (New York: Earthscan Publications, 2010), p. 213.
3 A. Miller and R. Hopkins, 'Climate after growth. Why environmentalists must embrace post-growth economics and community resilience', Post-Carbon Institute, September 2013.
4 This is no longer possible. See Thomas Piketty, *Capital in the Twenty-First Century*, trans. Arthur Goldhammer (Boston, MA: Harvard University Press, 2014); 'Le vrai rôle de l'énergie va obliger les économistes à changer de dogme', interview with Gaël Giraud published on 4 April 2014 on the blog http://petrole.blog.lemonde.fr/.
5 Jean-Pierre Dupuy, *Pour un catastrophisme éclairé: quand l'impossible est certain* (Paris: Seuil, 2002), pp. 84–5.
6 Hans Jonas, *The Imperative of Responsibility: In Search of an Ethics for the Technological Age* (Chicago, IL: University of Chicago Press, 1984).
7 Hamilton, *Requiem for a Species*, p. 179.
8 Christophe Bonneuil and Jean-Baptiste Fressoz, *L'Événement Anthropocène. La Terre, l'histoire et nous* (Paris: Seuil, 2013), p. 218.
9 Bonneuil and Fressoz, *L'Événement Anthropocène*, p. 359, note.
10 Bonneuil and Fressoz, *L'Événement Anthropocène*, p. 362, note.
11 Nicholas Georgescu-Roegen, *La Décroissance. Entropie, écologie, économie*, 3rd edn (Paris, Sang de la Terre et Ellébore, 2006).

12 Richard Heinberg, *The Party's Over: Oil, War and the Fate of Industrial Societies*, 2nd edn (Forest Rowe, East Sussex: Clairview Books, 2005).

For the Children

1 Gary Snyder, 'For the Children', *Turtle Island* (New York: New Directions, 1974), p. 86.